Assessment
Continuous Learning

LOIS BRIDGES

Stenhouse Publishers

The Galef Institute

Strategies for Teaching and Learning Professional Library

Administrators: Supporting School Change by Robert Wortman
Assessment: Continuous Learning by Lois Bridges
Creating Your Classroom Community by Lois Bridges
Drama as a Way of Knowing by Paul G. Heller
Math as a Way of Knowing by Susan Ohanian
Music as a Way of Knowing by Nick Page

Look for announcements of future titles in this series on dance, second language learners, literature, physical education, science, visual arts, and writing.

Stenhouse Publishers, 431 York Street, York, Maine 03909
The Galef Institute, 11050 Santa Monica Boulevard, Third Floor, Los Angeles, California 90025

Copyright © 1995 The Galef Institute.

Library of Congress Cataloging-in-Publication Data
Bridges, Lois
     Assessment : continuous learning / Lois Bridges.
       p.   cm. — (Strategies for teaching and learning professional library)
     Includes bibliographical references (p.).
     ISBN 1-57110-048-2 (alk. paper)
     1. Educational tests and measurements—Handbooks, manuals, etc.   2. Grading and marking (Students)—Handbooks, manuals, etc.   3. Portfolios in education—Handbooks, manuals, etc.   4. Learning—Handbooks, manuals, etc. I. Title.   II. Series.
     LB3051.B485 1995
     371.2'71—dc20
                                                 96-45751
                                                CIP

Manufactured in the United States of America on acid-free paper
01 00 99 98   8 7 6 5 4 3 2

Dear Colleague,

This is an exciting time for us to be educators.

Research across disciplines informs our understanding of human learning and development. We know how to support students as active, engaged learners in our classrooms. We know how to continuously assess student learning and development to make sensitive, instructional decisions. This is the art of teaching—knowing how to respond effectively at any given moment to our students' developmental needs.

As educators, we know that learning the art of teaching takes time, practice, and lots of professional support. To that end, the Strategies for Teaching and Learning Professional Library was developed. Each book invites you to explore theory (to know why) in the context of exciting teaching strategies (to know how) connected to evaluation of your students' learning as well as your own (to know you know). In addition, you'll find in-depth information about the unique rigors and challenges of each discipline, to help you make the most of the rich learning and teaching opportunities each discipline offers.

Use the books' *Dialogues* on your own and in the study groups to reflect upon your practices. The Dialogues invite responses to self-evaluative questions, experimentation with new instructional strategies in classrooms, and perhaps a rethinking of learning philosophy and classroom practices stimulated by new knowledge and understanding.

Shoptalks offer you lively reviews of the best and latest professional literature including professional journals and associations.

Teacher-To-Teacher Field Notes are full of tips and experiences from practicing educators who offer different ways of thinking about teaching practices and a wide range of classroom strategies they've found practical and successful.

As you explore and reflect on teaching and learning, we believe you'll continue to refine and extend your teaching art, and enjoy your professional life and the learning lives of your students.

Here's to the art of teaching!

Lois Bridges
Professional Development Editorial Director,
The Galef Institute

The Strategies for Teaching and Learning Professional Library is part of the Galef Institute's school reform initiative *Different Ways of Knowing*.

Different Ways of Knowing is a philosophy of education based on research in child development, cognitive theory, and multiple intelligences. It offers teachers, administrators, specialists, and other school and district educators continuing professional growth opportunities integrated with teaching and learning materials. The materials are supportive of culturally and linguistically diverse school populations and help all teachers and children to be successful. Teaching strategies focus on interdisciplinary, thematic instruction integrating history and social studies with the performing and visual arts, literature, writing, math, and science. Developed with the leadership of Senior Author Linda Adelman, *Different Ways of Knowing* has been field tested in hundreds of classrooms across the country.

For more information, write or call

The Galef Institute
11050 Santa Monica Boulevard, Third Floor, Los Angeles, California 90025
Tel 310.479.8883
Fax 310.473.9720

Strategies for Teaching and Learning Professional Library

Contributors

President
Linda Adelman

Vice President Programs and Communications
Sue Beauregard

Professional Development Editorial Director
Lois Bridges

Editor
Resa Gabe Nikol

Editorial Assistants
Elizabeth Finison, Wendy Sallin

Designers
Melvin Harris, Delfina Marquez-Noé,
Sarah McCormick, Jennifer Swan Myers,
Julie Suh

Photographers
Ted Beauregard, Dana Ross

For a year and a half, I learned side-by-side with 22 teachers and administrators involved in the Galef Assessment Project made possible by a generous contribution from the Ahmanson Foundation. Their thoughts, ideas, and insights are reflected throughout this text. I gratefully acknowledge their assistance and inspiration. Thanks also to Galef's Judy DeWitt and Karolynne Gee for helping to make this project a success.
—LB

Judy Bloomingdale-Vinke   Julie Friese   Mike McCoy   Gaye Petty

Judith Burchett   Judi Ibarra   Cynthia McNamara   Fay Powell

Helene Chirinian   Elizabeth Lutton   Nan Mohr   Noel Ray-Wysinger

Jean Diamond   Rosemarie Macias   David Moorhouse   Deborah Ventura

Nancy Gates   Carol Mahoney   Wendy Motoike

Sandy Glaser   Christina McCoy   Amy Perez

Special thanks to Andrew G. Galef and Bronya Pereira Galef for their continuing commitment to our nation's children and educators.

Contents

Chapter 1

Understanding Authentic Assessment

I'd like to introduce you to a second grade friend of mine. She's strong, she's wise, and she's seldom intimidated by anything. Recently, this friend of mine had to take the Iowa Test of Basic Skills and was quite perturbed with the whole experience. Not one to remain silent, she wrote a letter to the State Commissioner stating exactly how she felt.

Dear State Comm.,
I thought the Iowa Teast was trash. Cus I dint lean any thing If we dint do the Iowa Teast I would lean morr. I dint lean any thing cus my teacher said I can't tell you the answes. And on regler work my teacher comes around and looks at it and sas wats rong.

2nd grade

My friend is empowered! As a student, her focus is on learning—*continuous learning*. And continuous learning is the real power of assessment—or it should be. When we evaluate our students' learning or ask them to evaluate themselves, our primary goal should be to help them learn more.

Let's examine six underlying principles that define authentic assessment. These principles reveal how we can watch, listen, and learn from our students so that we may help them become more effective learners.

Six Defining Principles of Authentic Assessment

- Authentic assessment is continuous, informing every aspect of instruction and curriculum building. As they engage in authentic assessment, teachers discover and learn what to teach as well as how and when to teach it.
- Authentic assessment is an integral part of the curriculum. Children are assessed while they are involved with classroom learning experiences, not just before or after a unit through pre- or post-tests.
- Authentic assessment is developmentally and culturally appropriate.
- Authentic assessment focuses on students' strengths. Teachers assess what students *can* do, what they know, and how they can use what they know to learn.
- Authentic assessment recognizes that the most important evaluation is self-evaluation. Students and teachers need to understand why they are doing what they are doing so that they may have some sense of their own success and growth.
- Authentic assessment invites active collaboration; teachers, students, and parents work together to reflect and assess learning.

SHOPTALK

Goodman, Kenneth S., Lois Bridges Bird and Yetta M. Goodman, eds. *The Whole Language Catalog: Supplement on Authentic Assessment.* New York: SRA: Macmillan/McGraw-Hill, 1992.

What's inside for you?

Detailed explanations: developing and using authentic assessment, explaining it to parents and administrators, involving your students in self-evaluation, keeping track of and documenting your students' learning, and using the assessment data to plan instruction and build curriculum.

Evaluation tools: descriptive guides and forms for observing student learning, keeping anecdotal records, conducting teacher-parent-student conferences and interviews, and using holistic checklists, learning logs, portfolios, audio- and videotapes, and photographs.

In addition, you'll learn about developmental markers and how to document learning across the curriculum. The history of standardized testing is outlined, the problems inherent in these tests, and what you can do to work for more authentic forms of assessment.

Let's revisit each principle, illustrating each with examples from real teachers working in real classrooms.

Authentic assessment is continuous. Assessment doesn't just happen at the beginning or end of a semester. Every day teachers make mental or written notes about what and how their students are learning. Authentic assessment informs every aspect of instruction and curriculum building; teachers learn what to teach as well as how and when to teach it.

Authentic assessment is a two-way process. As we assess our students, we assess the effectiveness of our teaching. One way to assess students in authentic learning situations is by *kidwatching*. Kidwatching is defined simply as observing and listening to students during the course of a school day in order to learn more about their developmental needs and interests. Kidwatching informs our teaching. We learn what to teach and how to teach it, and when to revise our instructional strategies. The experiences of primary teacher Peter Jones (1987) illustrate the point. For several weeks, he carefully observed his student Joshua, eventually creating a profile of Joshua as a learner. Jones's kidwatching of Joshua was a major influence on his own growth and change as a teacher.

Jones writes:

> Our development has been complementary. I have learned from Joshua and he has learned from me. There was a cycle—Joshua made a minor development to which I responded in some positive way, resulting in Joshua's further improvement which provided me with reinforcement that my positive approach was working, which kept me watching…Hence the process continued, growing in momentum and finally involving not only Joshua, but the whole class.

Our students are mirrors reflecting back to us who we are as human beings and as teachers.

Field Notes: Teacher-To-Teacher

I find that my kidwatching journal is invaluable in helping me plan instruction that will really support my students. For example, I noticed that one of my students, Carlos, was resisting writing in his daily journal. I made a note of this in my kidwatching journal. Later that day, after the students had left, I revisited my notes and reflected on my observations of Carlos. After a moment of quiet reflection, I wrote:

"Sometimes I think kids feel they are not in control of their own writing and that they are writing for teachers, not for themselves. For Carlos, it seems important for him to realize he can write for himself and that it doesn't always have to be shared. I hope this will help him process some of the stuff that's going on with him."

Several days later, I talked with Carlos about the purpose of his journal and helped him to understand he could use it to write about things that he found personally meaningful. When next I was able to observe Carlos during journal time, I noted that he was using his journal again. And, as I had predicted, he was writing about issues he was grappling with at home.

My written observations of Carlos prompted me to carve out some time to consider his unique needs and to think about what I might do to support him. My observations and reflection enabled me to create a supportive instructional plan—time-out for a one-on-one conference with Carlos—that nudged him past his writing block. In this way, my observations support me as a responsive teacher.

Chris Castro
Fair Oaks Elementary School
Redwood City, California

Our students are mirrors reflecting back to us who we are as human beings and as teachers. They reveal to us what we believe about teaching and learning, and what we believe about our students. Through our students we can see clearly if what we are doing is working.

DIALOGUE

To test your tests—to evaluate their effectiveness as teaching-learning tools—ask yourself these questions.

Yes No

☐ ☐   Do the tests I give help me discover what to teach?

☐ ☐   Do the tests I give help me learn how to teach?

☐ ☐   Do the tests I give show me when I should teach?

Authentic assessment is an integral part of the curriculum. Children are assessed while they are involved with classroom learning experiences, not just before or after a unit through pre- or post-tests.

In general, watching, listening to, and interacting with our students while they are engaged in the daily flow of classroom learning yields more valid and helpful assessment data than isolated tests—particularly commercial tests that we haven't developed ourselves.

For example, how do you know when your students have become real readers? Think about your top readers. How do you know they are so capable? I bet if you composed a list of the ways you know, it would look something like this.

I know my students are real readers because

- they have favorite authors, illustrators, and books
- they know how to browse in a library or bookstore
- they talk about books with their friends
- they have library cards
- they know the names of local bookstores.

I bet your list didn't include a test score. That's because as informed teachers, our observations of our students' literate behaviors are more valid and reliable indicators of what it means to be a real reader than anything that currently exists on a test. We don't need a test to tell us when our kids are reading. As Dorothy Watson (1985) states eloquently, "Scores don't sharpen our vision or insight. They don't bring a smile or knowing nod. A score of 3.2 doesn't begin to describe a child's ability to use language."

SHOPTALK

Roderick, Jessie A., ed. *Context-Responsive Approaches to Assessing Children's Language.* Urbana, Illinois: National Council of Teachers of English, 1991.

"Assessment is a natural part of life and learning," writes Gay Su Pinnell in her chapter in this collection. This is perhaps the overarching theme of the book. Assessment that is "context-responsive," that captures and represents what students really know and what teachers are really doing, is necessarily tied to the daily life teachers and students share inside classrooms. Assessment must stem from the continuous learning and thinking in which students are engaged. The contributors to this book, all recognized scholars and practitioners in the field of literacy education and policy analysis, explore authentic assessment from three different perspectives: how it impacts classroom practice, what research has to say, and how policymakers might respond.

Authentic assessment is developmentally and culturally appropriate. Assessing children's growth is a careful, systematic process that takes place over time in many different contexts that are in constant flux. The process first occurs in the child's home language and is sensitive to cultural variations.

Maureen Morrissey, a primary bilingual teacher at Borton Primary Magnet School in Tucson, Arizona, greets her students the first day of school and asks them to wear name tags. Then she gives each child a questionnaire that is written in English on one side and Spanish on the other.

Find someone in the class who
- is the same height as you
- can read in Spanish and English, too
- can write the name of someone in class who wasn't in your class last year

- has the same size hand as you.

Busca a alguien en la clase que
- esté igual de alto que tu
- pueda leer en español y inglés también
- pueda escribir el nombre de alguien nuevo en tu clase que no estaba en esta clase el año pasado
- tenga las manos del mismo tamaño como tu.

Morrissey instructs the children to travel around the classroom, interview their classmates, and complete the questionnaire. She gives both English and

Spanish equal status, and she is able to quickly determine who has control over what language. She notices that David fills out the English side only; Jorge, the Spanish side; Ana answers all questions on both sides; and Manny answers one question only. An added bonus is that as the children interview each other, they become acquainted and begin to build the bonds that will unite them as a learning community over the course of the school year (Morrissey, 1989).

Authentic assessment focuses on students' strengths. In the clinical model of educational assessment, one looks for what is wrong with a child, and then writes a prescription to fix it. Authentic assessment invites us to find out what children know, how they can use what they know to learn, and what they can teach us. Children are natural learners in environments that seriously invite learning. When they have multiple ways to explore learning and multiple ways to show what they know, then all children shine as capable, creative learners.

Authentic assessment invites us to find out what children know, how they can use what they know to learn, and what they can teach us.

Let's explore the significance of shifting from diagnosing student weaknesses to celebrating student strengths by examining a note eight-year-old Mimi wrote her teacher, Diane Lohman, a primary teacher at Fair Oaks School in Redwood City, California. Mimi was upset that Lohman had failed to choose her for the class Busy Bee. She let Lohman know exactly how she felt.

If we were operating from a deficit model of learning, we would view Mimi's note as clear evidence of her complete misunderstanding of punctuation. We would pull out our favorite worksheets on punctuation and drill her on exclamation points. Next, we would test her on identical drills. If she passed the test, we could assure ourselves that we had taught her the exclamation point and could now declare her proficient (and if she failed the test, we'd simply give her additional drills and retest her).

On the other hand, as educators who understand how children construct knowledge, we can focus on Mimi's strengths as a language learner and celebrate all that she *does* know. Some of her strengths we might note include the following:

- Mimi is able to use language to protest; she understands the pragmatics of protest.
- She is aware that exclamation points denote emotion. She overgeneralizes punctuation exactly the way young children learning to talk will overgeneralize specific features of oral language (for example, past tense: *I goed to the park).*
- She substitutes *wat* for *want,* a typical pattern when children are learning to spell. Young children who rely on phonetic strategies for spelling omit features they don't hear or feel in their mouths or vocal chords; in this case, Mimi omits the silent preconsonantal nasal.

Field Notes: Teacher-To-Teacher

It seems so clear to me that the fill-in bubble form of assessment is a product of the industrial revolution. It sees students like a product on the assembly line. Authentic assessment is the humanization of our schools. We see children for the strengths they bring. We know more about what they've learned and what they are ready to learn than ever before.

Shannon Wilkins, Principal
Mark Twain Elementary School
Lawndale, California

Celebrating Mimi's strengths doesn't mean that we fail to address her overgeneralization of the exclamation point. But let's consider instructional appropriateness. We need to honor Mimi's passionate message. Using her impassioned note to teach her the function of exclamation points would be missing the point. Better to respond (immediately!) to her message, note the overgeneralization in our kidwatching records, and later pull Mimi aside, perhaps with her classmates who need similar instruction, and do a quick minilesson on exclamation points. We can begin by inviting Mimi to notice how published authors use exclamation points. We can explain that this form of punctuation is used sparingly to denote strong emotion. By demonstrating their use in our own writing and in the published materials available in the classroom, we can help Mimi understand how exclamation points work without undermining her self-confidence as a language learner. Clearly, Mimi believes in herself as a writer and doesn't hesitate to put pen to paper when life demands it. We celebrate her enthusiasm and strengths. And we nudge her forward in her understanding of the finer points of language when it's appropriate.

SHOPTALK

Johnston, Peter H. *Knowing Literacy: Constructive Literacy Assessment.* York, Maine: Stenhouse Publishers, 1997.

Peter Johnston writes, "Assessment…is a profoundly human, social phenomenon, thoroughly value-laden." While Johnston offers a dozen practical ways to assess children's development across the literacy spectrum—reading, writing and spelling—he also challenges his readers to consider why they are assessing, what they are assessing, and how they will use their assessment data to help their students flourish and learn. This remarkable book meets the every day assessment needs of classroom teachers at the same time it encourages teachers to continually rethink and refine their assessment practices.

Students and teachers need to understand why they are doing what they are doing so they may have some sense of their own success and growth.

Authentic assessment recognizes that the most important evaluation is self-evaluation. Students and teachers need to understand why they are doing what they are doing so that they may have some sense of their own success and growth.

There are those like Courtney Cazden of Harvard University whom I've heard speak at teachers' conferences, who believe that the very essence of education is self-reflection—the ability to step outside of a learning experience and evaluate: "What is working for me? What's not working? What can I do to make it work?" With awareness comes power, the ability to monitor, document, and control one's own learning.

Field Notes: Teacher-To-Teacher

Evaluation is a natural part of the growth process. You can't get where you're going (reach your goal), if you don't know where you are. Self-evaluation is the key to reaching goals, and it is what the child thinks of his or her own work that really matters in development.

Jean Diamond
Muscatel Middle School
Rosemead, California

Rena Malkofsky is an elementary school teacher at El Carmelo School in Palo Alto, California. Her students keep learning logs for every subject. They write their way into understanding across the curriculum. One day, when Malkofsky was giving a lesson on long division, she noticed that many of her students had a glazed look in their eyes. Was it boredom? lack of understanding? indifference? Malkofsky decided to find out. "Get out your math logs," she instructed her students, "and explain what long division is." This is Stella's explanation. What do you think; did Stella get it?

> Division is like disecting an animal, but insted you disect a #. I use division when I try to figure out the math puzzle. I think Division is like fractions except for me it is harder.

Malkofsky's students have learned that it's not enough to just get the right answer. You have to understand how you got it.

Malkofsky tells this story: Every week, her students must solve a new "Problem of the Week" (POW). They have to show their calculations in their math learning log, and they must also explain how they went about finding their solution. One day, Malkofsky overheard a conversation between Jacob and Noah. Jacob had discovered the correct answer to the POW, so Noah, who was struggling with the problem, asked him for help. "Hang on, Noah," Malkofsky heard Jacob say. "I know I've got the answer, but I don't understand how I got it. Let me do some writing, figure it out, and as soon as I understand it, I'll help you."

Schoolchildren are never too young to engage in self-evaluation. At Orion School in Redwood City, California, primary teacher Pam Anderson asks her five and six year olds to complete a self-evaluation form, the "Primary Developmental Checklist." She introduces the form the second week of school, and helps the children think about the things they can do and the things they want to learn. Each child then chooses three goals on which to work—a social, academic, and physical goal. School begins with a 20 minute goal-working session. Children enter the classroom and get right to work on their goals. Once they've completed their chosen goals, they choose three more. As Anderson explains, "It's very exciting, by the end of the year, for the children to have completed all the goals on the form!"

Primary Developmental Checklist

Name _____ Date_____ Grade _____

Personal Information and Other Learning Skills

I know my address. ☐ yes ☐ not yet	I know my telephone number. ☐ yes ☐ not yet	I know my age and birthdate. ☐ yes ☐ not yet	I can write my first and last name. ☐ yes ☐ not yet
I can tie my shoes. ☐ yes ☐ not yet	I know my right and left hand. ☐ yes ☐ not yet	I know the names of these shapes. ☐ yes ☐ not yet	I know the parts of my body. ☐ yes ☐ not yet
I can cut on a line. ☐ yes ☐ not yet	I know upper and lower case letters of the alphabet. ☐ yes ☐ not yet	I can print upper and lower case letters. ☐ yes ☐ not yet	I know and use the scientific method. ☐ yes ☐ not yet

Social Skills and Work Habits

I keep my hands to myself. ☐ yes ☐ not yet	I listen when others are speaking. ☐ yes ☐ not yet	I am a good speaker before a group. ☐ yes ☐ not yet	I can solve my own problems. ☐ yes ☐ not yet
I cooperate with others. ☐ yes ☐ not yet	I take turns and share. ☐ yes ☐ not yet	I help others. ☐ yes ☐ not yet	I put things away. ☐ yes ☐ not yet

The Whole Language Catalog: Forms for Authentic Assessment © 1994 edited by Lois Bridges Bird, Kenneth S. Goodman and Yetta M. Goodman

Primary Developmental Checklist

More Work Habits

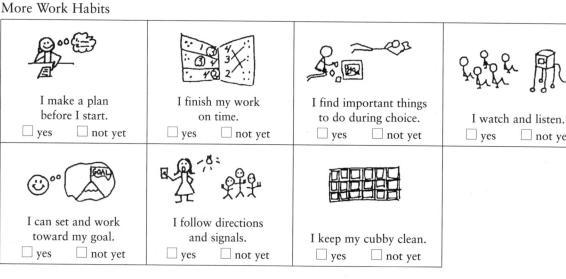

I make a plan before I start. ☐ yes ☐ not yet	I finish my work on time. ☐ yes ☐ not yet	I find important things to do during choice. ☐ yes ☐ not yet	I watch and listen. ☐ yes ☐ not yet
I can set and work toward my goal. ☐ yes ☐ not yet	I follow directions and signals. ☐ yes ☐ not yet	I keep my cubby clean. ☐ yes ☐ not yet	

Physical Education Skills

I can jump rope. ☐ yes ☐ not yet	I can catch a ball. ☐ yes ☐ not yet	I can skip. ☐ yes ☐ not yet	I can bounce a ball. ☐ yes ☐ not yet
I can hop. ☐ right foot ☐ left foot ☐ yes ☐ not yet	I can jump rope backwards. ☐ yes ☐ not yet	I can balance. ☐ yes ☐ not yet	I can throw a ball. ☐ yes ☐ not yet
I can throw a frisbee. ☐ yes ☐ not yet	I can throw a football. ☐ yes ☐ not yet	I'm a good sport. ☐ yes ☐ not yet	I can run the baseball diamond. ☐ yes ☐ not yet
I can do sit ups. ☐ yes ☐ not yet	I can do jumping jacks. ☐ yes ☐ not yet	I have the strength to cross the traveling bar. ☐ yes ☐ not yet	

The Whole Language Catalog: Forms for Authentic Assessment © 1994 edited by Lois Bridges Bird, Kenneth S. Goodman and Yetta M. Goodman

Primary Developmental Checklist

Math Skills

I can draw these shapes. ☐ yes ☐ not yet	I recognize patterns. ☐ yes ☐ not yet	I can sort. ☐ yes ☐ not yet	I can count ___ objects. ☐ yes ☐ not yet
I can count by 1's (to 127). ☐ yes ☐ not yet	I can count by 2's (to 106). ☐ yes ☐ not yet	I can count by 5's (to 125). ☐ yes ☐ not yet	I can count by 10's (to 120). ☐ yes ☐ not yet
Favorite Fruit I can read a graph. ☐ yes ☐ not yet	I can match sets. ☐ yes ☐ not yet	I can make a pattern. ☐ yes ☐ not yet	I can make a graph. ☐ yes ☐ not yet
$3+4=7$ $1+8=9$ $\begin{array}{r} 2 \\ +2 \\ \hline 4 \end{array}$ I can do addition to 10. ☐ yes ☐ not yet	$10-5=5$ $6-4=2$ $\begin{array}{r} 3 \\ -2 \\ \hline 1 \end{array}$ I can do subtraction from 10. ☐ yes ☐ not yet	Incredible equations: $10-2=8$ $3+5=8$ $2+2+2+2=8$ I can give number sentences. ☐ yes ☐ not yet	I can recognize and count money. ☐ yes ☐ not yet
I can read and use the calendar. ☐ yes ☐ not yet	I can tell time. ☐ yes ☐ not yet	$3+2=5$ I can write number sentences. ☐ yes ☐ not yet	16 3 11 7 4 12 6 20 5 18 15 I can recognize numbers 0–20. ☐ yes ☐ not yet
TENS ONES! 3 5 I can build a double- digit number. ☐ yes ☐ not yet	HUNDREDS TENS ONES 1 2 4 I can build a triple- digit number. ☐ yes ☐ not yet	$5>3$ $2<7$ $4>1$ $61<62$ I know and use > and < signs. ☐ yes ☐ not yet	83 65 31 92 77 29 I can recognize random 2-digit numbers. ☐ yes ☐ not yet

The Whole Language Catalog: Forms for Authentic Assessment © 1994 edited by Lois Bridges Bird, Kenneth S. Goodman and Yetta M. Goodman

Primary Developmental Checklist

Reading Skills

Sh r T S h Ch B Th I know beginning consonant sounds. ☐ yes ☐ not yet	ă ĕ ĭ ŏ ŭ I know short vowel sounds. ☐ yes ☐ not yet	ā ē ī ō ū I know long vowel sounds. ☐ yes ☐ not yet	I can sound out. ☐ yes ☐ not yet
I can skip and go on. ☐ yes ☐ not yet	I can give a good substitute word. ☐ yes ☐ not yet	I know punctuation marks. ☐ yes ☐ not yet	I can read aloud with expression. ☐ yes ☐ not yet
I know the characters in a story. ☐ yes ☐ not yet	I know the setting in a story. ☐ yes ☐ not yet	I know the plot in a story. ☐ yes ☐ not yet	I read alone during silent reading. ☐ yes ☐ not yet
I participate in literature study discussions. ☐ yes ☐ not yet	I finish my literature study homework. ☐ yes ☐ not yet		

Writing Skills

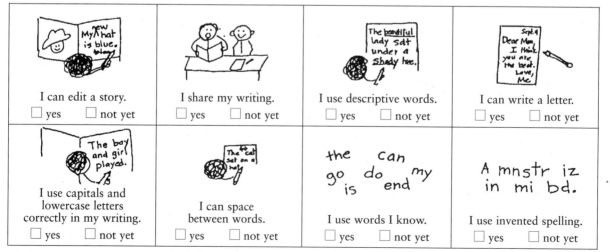

I can edit a story. ☐ yes ☐ not yet	I share my writing. ☐ yes ☐ not yet	I use descriptive words. ☐ yes ☐ not yet	I can write a letter. ☐ yes ☐ not yet
I use capitals and lowercase letters correctly in my writing. ☐ yes ☐ not yet	I can space between words. ☐ yes ☐ not yet	I use words I know. ☐ yes ☐ not yet	I use invented spelling. ☐ yes ☐ not yet

The Whole Language Catalog: Forms for Authentic Assessment © 1994 edited by Lois Bridges Bird, Kenneth S. Goodman and Yetta M. Goodman

Authentic assessment invites active collaboration; teachers, students, and parents work together to reflect and assess learning. Students are valued as unique, thoughtful individuals who can participate in evaluating their progress. Teachers and students are co-learners, working together to plan, monitor, and assess all learning experiences. Parents become learning partners, too.

Debra Goodman, who teaches at the Dewey Learning Center in inner city Detroit, begins the school year by thinking about and listing what she wants her students to experience and accomplish by year's end. She shares her goals with her students and asks them to spend some time thinking about what they want to accomplish. They list their goals under hers. Then she sends both lists home and asks parents to respond and write their goals. In this way, all learning partners are apprised of each other's goals. Several times throughout the year, all partners revisit the goals and revise them as needed.

Here is a partial list of Goodman's goals, Heather's goals, and Heather's dad's response.

Students are valued as unique, thoughtful individuals who can participate in evaluating their progress.

My Goals for My Students
- Learn to work together and help others
- Learn to solve problems and think for themselves
- Learn to organize work and take responsibility for their own work
- Improve their communication in speaking and writing
- Learn some steps in doing research
- Find some books and authors they love
- Have an idea of what history is
- Learn about many different cultures
- Learn more about their own family history and culture

> Student Goals
> My Goals for 5th Grade:
>
> Try to get better grades this year
> Write better cursive
> Talk much less
> Be a better student
> Be more to myself.
> Dress better.
> Get along with family
> By the end of year I plan to have long hair
>
> Heather Kirkland
> Student Signature
>
> Parents: Please comment and return.
>
> These are my daughter's goals and we the members of her family are certainly going to work hard with her to try to achieve them so that she can accomplish as many of them as possible.
>
> Father: Henderson Kirkland

Assessment is part of the continuous flow of life. We assess continuously; in fact, assessment may be related to what it means to be human.

New evaluation strategics that embrace our well-researched new understandings of language and learning are variously known as *authentic assessment*, *performance-based assessment*, and *alternative assessment* (no longer thought of as alternative). Yetta Goodman's 1978 coinage is perhaps most basic and direct: *kidwatching*.

Regardless of what we choose to call it, authentic assessment is something we all know how to do. Indeed, assessment is part of the continuous flow of life. We assess continuously; in fact, assessment may be related to what it means to be human. We are constantly stepping back from our experience and evaluating our actions, our thoughts, our feelings. What seems to be working for us? What isn't working as well?

It's exactly this sort of on-the-spot assessment—not separate from the flow of classroom life—that we, as teachers, engage in constantly. Ask any teacher about any student in his or her class, and almost certainly the teacher will talk at length about the student, discussing the child from multiple perspectives: personal, social, and academic. Most teachers are keen, sensitive observers of their students and respond to each student somewhat differently based on their professional and personal understandings of each student's personality and academic needs and strengths. Teachers don't evaluate the isolated, concrete knowledge their students may possess at a given point in time. Rather, effective teachers assess frequently over time, looking at the full spectrum of their students' understanding. They note how their students use a range of learning strategies in a variety of contexts, how they make connections to their own experiences, and how they apply new understandings in meaningful and novel ways.

DIALOGUE

Think about the ways you learn with and from your students. Think about the six defining principles of authentic assessment.

In what ways do I already practice authentic assessment in my classroom?

_____

_____

Which principles do I feel comfortable with?

_____

_____

Which ones would I like to develop?

_____

_____

How might I accomplish my goals?

_____

_____

Continuous Professional Growth

We need to believe in ourselves as professionals, and trust our own professional senses about our students. And we also need to constantly upgrade our professionalism by keeping abreast of professional literature, attending conferences, and initiating lively discussions with our colleagues about teaching and learning. As we become better kidwatchers, we become more effective, responsive educators. We can refine our professional awareness and hone our kidwatching skills by

- becoming consciously aware of the natural, spontaneous kidwatching we do and use it as valid, helpful assessment data
- becoming more systematic in our kidwatching strategies, beginning to monitor how, when, and what we observe
- increasing our theoretical understanding of learning, language, and different ways of knowing
- knowing our students as individuals with unique needs and interests
- understanding the social-political nature of the communities in which we teach
- engaging in continuous self-reflection and evaluation of our teaching.

S H O P T A L K

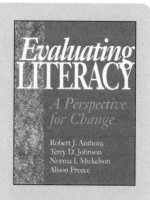

Anthony, Robert J., Terry D. Johnson, Norma I. Mickelson and Alison Preece. *Evaluating Literacy: A Perspective for Change.* Portsmouth, New Hampshire: Heinemann, 1991.

For school faculties attempting to adopt a system of evaluation that embraces learner-centered education, this book will serve as a valuable guide. Well organized and succinct, the authors provide readers with both the theory underlying authentic assessment and the practical wherewithal needed to put theory into practice. The first two chapters outline the basic principles of authentic assessment and the myths surrounding traditional evaluative measures. Chapters 3 and 4 present a model of assessment. Chapter 5 addresses the role of parents. The remaining chapters tackle the nuts and bolts of making it all work in the classroom. The authors succeed in their aim to present "evaluation strategies that can be easily and successfully implemented."

Chapter 2

We Assess To Learn and Teach

Peter H. Johnston reports in his book *Knowing Literacy* (1997), that teachers in one school district objected to the standardized tests they were required to administer yearly at every grade level. The teachers argued that the tests took valuable time from instruction, that they were expensive, and that they adversely affected teaching. The teachers requested a Board of Education meeting where they made one simple request, that the Board respond to the question "What do you need from our district's assessment system?" It was an important question, but not easy to answer. After much deliberation, the Board listed the primary purposes of assessment:

- to document children's development
- to make sure some children don't accidentally "miss the boat"
- to keep students apprised of their progress
- to keep the public informed
- to make sure that the district is held to high standards.

In their list, the Board discovered the essence of authentic assessment. They recognized that assessment makes sense only if it helps teachers, students, parents, and all those involved in the educational process—that assessment separate from instruction is of little value. When we engage in authentic assessment, teaching, learning, and evaluation are all linked. Each informs and shapes the other.

This, then, is the real power of assessment—it informs our teaching practice. It tells us if what we're doing is working with our students. It helps us ensure that our students won't "miss the boat." In fact, there are those who have suggested that the acid test of evaluation should be, "Does it help us know how and what and when to teach (Crafton 1991)?" In other words, when we evaluate our students' learning or ask them to evaluate themselves, our primary goal should be to help them learn more.

When we evaluate our students' learning or ask them to evaluate themselves, our primary goal should be to help them learn more.

DIALOGUE

What does evaluation mean to me?

_____

_____

Why do I evaluate?

_____

_____

What do I do with the evaluative data I collect?

_____

_____

How do I use the data?

_____

_____

How do I share it?

_____

_____

The most effective teaching is responsive. Responding in a sensitive and supportive manner begins with knowing your students. As you come to understand your students' developmental needs and gain insight into their interests and concerns, you'll know what, how, and when to teach. Authentic assessment and kidwatching are learning tools which enable you to know your students as learners. Kidwatching helps you become a more effective, responsive teacher.

Field Notes: Teacher-To-Teacher

To me, evaluation is a way of checking what students are learning and how they are learning. It helps me see if the classroom contexts are helping them progress. It shows me student strengths and problem areas. It shows me if I'm reaching students or if I need to reteach something in a different way.

Christina McCoy
Roosevelt Elementary School
Lawndale, California

In keeping with our understanding that effective evaluation informs instruction, opportunities for kidwatching are built into *Different Ways of Knowing* and enable you to achieve multiple assessment goals. You'll discover

- how your students are learning; the strategies and skills they use to learn
- what your students are learning; their growing understanding and knowledge of key social studies concepts
- how to document your students' learning growth; and, equally important, how to help them become self-reflective learners who can monitor and document their own learning
- how to plan and revise your instruction and curriculum based on the kidwatching data you collect and analyze.

In *Different Ways of Knowing*, learning, teaching, and evaluation are fully integrated. Each learning event is organized around a three-part cycle:

- Coming To Know: The Process of Learning
- Showing You Know: The Products of Learning
- Knowing You Know: Reflections

This cycle follows the natural progression of human learning and serves as a framework through which to view and assess student progress.

There are a variety of ways to document the kidwatching data you collect. *Different Ways of Knowing* includes three kidwatching forms which correspond to each part of the learning cycle: "Coming To Know," "Showing You Know," and "Knowing You Know." There is also a form that children can use for self-reflection. We recommend keeping one of each form for each student (three forms per student).

A three-ring, loose-leaf notebook with a section for each student is a convenient way to organize the kidwatching data. You may want to record two or three observations of the process, products, and reflections of each student through the learning cycle, noting how they learn, what they learn, and how they reflect on their own learning. In this way, you'll have recorded kidwatching data on each of the three forms for every student.

You may find other alternative ways to document kidwatching data helpful.

- Use the forms to help you identify what to watch for, but do your actual recording on blank sheets of paper. Later, you can select the most significant observations and record them on the forms, or simply highlight them on the separate sheets with a highlighter pen, reserving the forms for reference only.
- Mailing labels or self-stick notes offer a convenient way to collect your kidwatching data. As you spot a noteworthy event, record it on a mailing label or self-stick note. At your convenience, transfer the label to the *Different Ways of Knowing* kidwatching form.

Coming To Know: The Process of Learning

In this first part of the learning cycle, students acquire and process new information. The focus, then, is on how students come to know. Are they able to use their prior knowledge to make sense of new experiences? What skills and strategies do they use as they work to solve problems and answer questions? As you observe and monitor your students' learning, you will want to note their

Engagement

- pleasure—confidence and involvement in the learning event
- perseverance—working for extended periods of time
- risk-taking—curiosity and inventiveness

- responsibility—effective use of time; completing projects in a timely way

Collaboration

- ability to share ideas and opinions with peers, teacher, and other adults
- willingness to seek and respond to feedback from peers, teacher, and other adults
- willingness to use input from peers or teacher
- ability to undertake a task for and with a group

Flexibility

- ability to explore and use multiple learning modalities
- exercising options, moving from one modality to another
- problem solving; using many resources in search for answers to questions
- willingness to revise; deciding how, when, and why changes should be made.

When students can show what they know to themselves and to others, they and their teachers have a real sense of what has been learned.

Showing You Know: The Products of Learning

When students can show what they know to themselves and to others, they are given the chance to construct their own knowledge and their teachers have a real sense of what has been learned. The focus, then, is on the products of learning which may include written compositions as well as presentations that highlight the visual and performing arts.

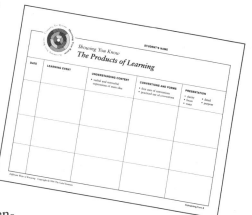

You'll want to note your students' understanding of content, uses of conventions and forms, and effectiveness of presentation.

Understanding Content

Is the student able to identify and express main ideas?

Conventions and Forms

Does the student show a desire to learn to use—and practice using—standard conventions and forms in all modes of expression? For example, in writing—spelling, punctuation, paragraphing, capitalization, grammar; in visual art—balance, repetition, contrast, unity, theme; in dance—time, space, shape, direction, level, energy; and so on.

Presentation

- clarity—Is the information presented in a logical manner? Can the audience follow the presenter's line of thought?
- focus—Does the piece focus on the message, every element supporting and advancing the main point?
- voice—Does the audience hear an individual human speak from the piece? Voice pulls the audience into the piece; the energy of the voice sparks the audience's attention and holds its interest.

Detail

Audiences crave specifics. Does the presenter include a depth and breadth of information such as quotations, facts, concrete details, observations, anecdotes, and images?

Purpose

Does the presenter have and meet an objective? What does the audience need to know? What will interest them? What can the audience use? What will surprise the audience?

Knowing You Know: Reflections

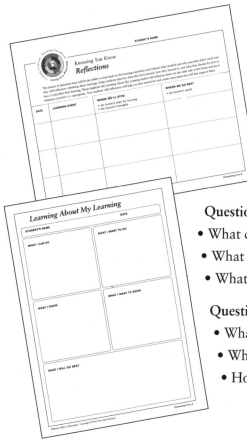

The essence of education may well be the ability to look back on the learning experience and evaluate what worked and why, and what didn't work and why. Self-reflection—or knowing you know—helps students discover what they have learned, how they learned it, and what they should do next to extend and refine their learning. Your students' self-reflections will help you plan instruction and create curriculum that will best support them.

Questions for the Learner

- What can I do? What do I want to do?
- What do I know? What do I want to know?
- What will I do next?

Questions for the Teacher

- What strengths does the learner have?
- What needs does the learner have?
- How can I help?

Coming To Know
The Process of Learning

STUDENT'S NAME

DATE	LEARNING EVENT	ENGAGEMENT • pleasure and involvement • perseverance • risk-taking • responsibility	COLLABORATION • thoughts expressed • openness to feedback • use of input • group work	FLEXIBILITY • modalities used • problem-solving strategies • revision strategies

Different Ways of Knowing © 1994 The Galef Institute

Kidwatching Form **1**

Showing You Know
The Products of Learning

STUDENT'S NAME

DATE	LEARNING EVENT	UNDERSTANDING CONTENT • verbal and nonverbal expressions of main idea	CONVENTIONS AND FORMS • first uses of conventions • practiced use of conventions	PRESENTATION • clarity • detail • focus • purpose • voice

Different Ways of Knowing © 1994 The Galef Institute

Kidwatching Form **2**

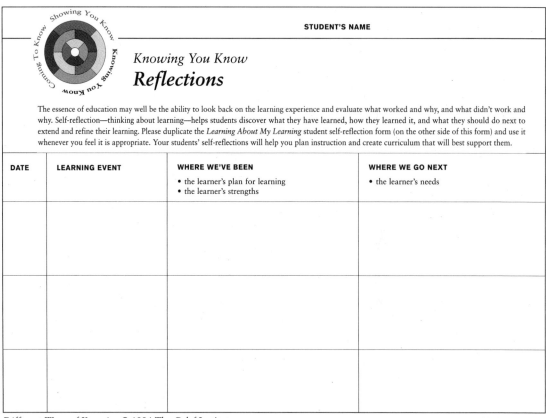

STUDENT'S NAME

Knowing You Know
Reflections

The essence of education may well be the ability to look back on the learning experience and evaluate what worked and why, and what didn't work and why. Self-reflection—thinking about learning—helps students discover what they have learned, how they learned it, and what they should do next to extend and refine their learning. Please duplicate the *Learning About My Learning* student self-reflection form (on the other side of this form) and use it whenever you feel it is appropriate. Your students' self-reflections will help you plan instruction and create curriculum that will best support them.

DATE	LEARNING EVENT	WHERE WE'VE BEEN • the learner's plan for learning • the learner's strengths	WHERE WE GO NEXT • the learner's needs

Different Ways of Knowing © 1994 The Galef Institute

Kidwatching Form **3**

Learning About My Learning

STUDENT'S NAME   **DATE**

WHAT I CAN DO

WHAT I WANT TO DO

WHAT I KNOW

WHAT I WANT TO KNOW

WHAT I WILL DO NEXT

Different Ways of Knowing © 1994 The Galef Institute

Kidwatching Form **4**

Five Kidwatching Perspectives

During the learning cycle—Coming To Know, Showing You Know, and Knowing You Know—as we work to understand our students and their developmental needs and interests, we may assume five kidwatching perspectives (Bridges Bird, Goodman and Goodman 1994).

1. Monitoring: Keeping Track
2. Observing: What's Going On?
3. Interacting: Finding Out
4. Analyzing Artifacts: Delving Deeper
5. Reporting: Summing Up

I discuss the kidwatching perspectives separately, but in most cases when you'll use them, they are overlapping and integrated. Each can help confirm the information gained from the others. I'll briefly explain each using real classroom examples, developed by real teachers, with real kids.

S H O P T A L K

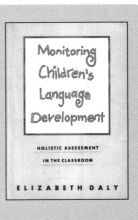

Daly, Elizabeth, ed. *Monitoring Children's Language Development: Holistic Assessment in the Classroom.* Portsmouth, New Hampshire: Heinemann, 1990.

This collection of 13 essays by Australia's leading language educators outlines the evaluation strategies that are compatible with constructivist learning theory. The first section, "Assessment for Learning: What Does It Mean?" explains the critical role of evaluation in curriculum development and responsive instruction. I found especially helpful Barbara Comber's chapter, "The Learner as Informant," in which she suggests ways to help teachers become researchers in their own classrooms, taking their instructional and curricular cues from their students. The second section, "Assessment in Practice," takes readers into classrooms, primary through secondary, mainstream as well as special education, and addresses the concerns that inevitably arise in the classroom: how to involve students in self-evaluation, how to report progress to parents, how to observe students' learning and interpret the results, and how to create student learning profiles. To the long list of invaluable learner-centered exports from our neighbors down under—add this book!

1. Monitoring: Keeping Track

The first focus is keeping track. During the course of a school day, students participate in many different learning experiences. We need to find ways to track them all. For example, for teachers and students using *Different Ways of Knowing,* there are multiple aspects to monitor. What learning events have students experienced? Which research materials have they used? Which learning modalities did they explore? Teachers devise a great many ways of keeping track of their students' learning experiences with checklists, inventories, and class lists. Children should also be involved and can account for their learning day through journal entries and lists. Over the course of a year, teachers and students can keep track of and compile a substantial record of learning experiences and accomplishments.

D I A L O G U E

How do I keep track of my students' learning experiences?

_____

_____

What do I keep track of?

_____

_____

How do I involve my students in keeping track of their own learning experiences?

_____

_____

_____

---

2. Observing: What's Going On?

Thoughtful observation of students at work and active listening to student talk is part of effective teaching. When Marty Morgenbesser (1991), a primary teacher in Sebastopol, California, came to realize that good teaching meant watching and listening to his students, he learned to take his instructional cues from his students, rather than follow scripted lesson plans. He explains his discovery.

When you come right down to it, teaching is improvisational theater. Unfortunately, most of us are trained in classical acting. We learn our lines to the letter, plan the blocking precisely, don our masks, and deliver our soliloquies. We might as well be Hamlet talking to poor Yorick's skull. Real teaching occurs the moment we stop delivering our lines and listen to others. As in improvisational acting (and in life for that matter), we have a general idea of the scene, but we don't know the lines until they leave our lips. What we say depends as much on what others say as it does on what we think we're going to say. So we'd better well listen.

Here's a little experience that Morgenbesser had that perfectly illustrates his point. He was teaching a group of seven and eight year olds to build two-digit numbers with base-ten blocks. He asked Anna to construct the number 96. Normally, this would entail placing nine ten-value sticks to the left of six sticks each with a value of one.

Anna reached for the 100-value block and, as Morgenbesser puts it, he reached for his "teacher mask." "Are you sure you need a hundred block, Anna?" She confidently replied, "I want to do it a different way" and Morgenbesser very tentatively agreed. Anna proceeded to place a 100-value block in the middle, flanked by one ten on the left and six ones on the right. "See, it's like a Roman numeral!—XCIIIIII."

Morgenbesser said he was "floored." Just earlier that morning, Anna had appeared to be confused by Roman numerals. Now, not only did she demonstrate an understanding of the concept, she was able to apply her new knowledge in a very creative way. By the way, she also demonstrated that she could represent the problem in the "regular way" as well.

Morgenbesser concludes this little vignette by saying, "My teacher's mask, dangling just below the chin, slipped off and shattered. Without that mask, I find that I hear much better."

We can gather valuable information about our students as learners by observing and listening. We may choose to observe one student working alone, a student as a member of a group, all members of a small group, or the class as a whole. We may record our general impressions or use observation to confirm or reject specific notions regarding the students. Some teachers find setting aside a specific period of time daily for systematic observation of individual students is the most effective way to handle this strategy; others keep a clipboard on hand for continuous note-taking as they see things happen that are worth recording. There is no one right way to engage in kidwatching. Explore several approaches and find the one that works best for you and your students. Chapter 3 addresses specific kidwatching strategies.

3. Interacting: Finding Out

Interacting with students during the learning process enables us to discover what our students know, feel, and believe, and to challenge them to explore beyond what they are thinking and feeling at the moment. We can question our students informally during class or small-group discussions. We can also question them one-on-one through their journals, or a more formal interview. Teachers interact with their students most effectively when they listen patiently and reflectively, and ask thoughtful, open-ended questions that nudge children to examine their own thinking: Why do you think so? Is it possible? What if we tried this instead? What if I said... ? I wonder if... ?

We can gather valuable information about our students as learners by observing and listening.

To illustrate the learning potential of teacher-student interaction, I'd like to tell you a story about my good friend Gloria Norton. Norton is the former resource teacher of Fair Oaks School, a whole language, bilingual school in Redwood City, California. She has worked with kids for more than thirty years. She is a talented whole language teacher and a sensitive kidwatcher. As the resource teacher, she often worked with kids who seemed to be falling between the cracks in their classrooms. One such child was Paul. It was late November when Norton began to work with him. He was in second grade and was still producing letter strings in his journal.

Through traditional instructional approaches, Norton would have started him on a series of handwriting and phonics worksheets—

Paul   NOV 30

IToYtITOUtoOVLoT.ob
Yo UTobPUtoPUToP UT
toUT OUTOQ UT.OQ
U TOQUTOP UTOQOPNoP LP
YTSOPQToP

first the initial consonants, then the final consonants, long vowels, short vowels, blends, digraphs, and schwas. Instead, she engaged him in written conversations, a technique developed by Professor Carolyn Burke of the University of Indiana. Norton responded to all of Paul's attempts to write as meaningful. He would write using his pretend writing, explain what it said, and Norton would write a response. After several weeks of corresponding in this way, Norton, as a sensitive kidwatcher, knew that Paul could do more. All he needed was a gentle nudge, and so she said, "Paul, I want you to write so that I can read it." The results were instantaneous and dramatic. Paul became a writer, able to use written language to communicate with others (*Becoming a Whole Language School: The Fair Oaks Story.* Bridges Bird 1991).

Paul   Dec 17

mly Bist fin is Antonio
We Like ehi ararr
We Pla agt The Prk
wih MY hraks

Paul, this is great! I can read the whole thing! What is your favorite thing to do in school? Mrs. N

I Like Mih^math Bist

I bet you'll like journals too, you're doing so well

DIALOGUE

While most educators agree with the value inherent in interacting one-on-one with students, many feel overwhelmed at the thought of finding time to sit down and interview each student. Even a fifteen-minute interview, multiplied thirty times, may seem impossible.

How can I organize the day to create time to interact one-on-one with my students?

_____

What are my other students doing while I'm talking with one student?

_____

Do I formally interview each student? Do I tape the interview? What sorts of questions do I ask?

_____

What do I do with the information I acquire from interviews, interest inventories, questionnaires?

_____

What other ways have I found to interact one-on-one with students: through dialogue journals, home visits, with parent help, or cross-age tutors?

_____

4. Analyzing Artifacts: Delving Deeper

The fourth kidwatching perspective centers on collecting and analyzing in greater depth the artifacts of learning such as written stories and reports, sketches and drawings, or videotapes of students' presentations, dances, or dramatic productions. These provide students, parents, other teachers, and administrators with concrete evidence of progress.

As you examine artifacts of children's learning, it's best to consider both content and process. Focusing only on the final product can be misleading. For example, one teacher was concerned when she observed her young student's drawing of a truck. On its side he had written Mayflower backwards.

Although young children need time to explore and learn the conventions that govern the directionality of written language, teachers and parents alike can grow concerned if children persist in reversing their letters and words. In this case, rather than assuming there was a problem, the teacher simply asked her student how he happened to draw the truck the way he had. He responded, "You know when you see a truck flying down a hill, the letters zip by like this." Similar thinking prompted Marisela to write her dialogue backwards in one of her dialogue balloons because after all, "I'm having a conversation with my aunt." Unless we interact with our students and observe the process of their work, we may miss the wonderful logic that governs their exploration of the world (Y. Goodman 1991).

As we evaluate the artifacts of our students' learning, we need to have established specific criteria that we use to guide our evaluation. Many effective educators involve their students in negotiating and helping to establish the criteria. When students debate and discuss the standards of excellence, then they can consciously strive to achieve those standards in their own work.

Field Notes: Teacher-To-Teacher

Evaluation information should be shared with anyone who affects the child's development as a learner, especially the child! Family involvement is attained by familiarizing students and families with the evaluation process and inviting their input and suggestions to help validate the process.

Judith Burchett
Rogers Middle School
Lawndale, California

Nan Bonfils is an elementary teacher at the International School of Kuala Lumpur in Malaysia. She has found that engaging her students in a dialogue about effective writing is valuable in helping them understand the qualities of effective writing. Bonfils selects four papers from other classrooms that span a range of quality. The papers are anonymous; she labels them W, X, Y, and Z. Bonfils gives each student photocopies of all four. She follows this procedure as she helps her students establish criteria for effective writing:

- Together as a class they read each paper out loud without comment.
- Students reread the papers silently and sort them into two piles—"ones I like and ones I don't like." Rule: you have to have at least one paper in each pile.
- Students work independently to refine their sorting and rank the papers one to four "with a score of four going to the best and one to the one you didn't like at all."
- Students explain in writing their reasons for ranking; in other words, "What makes paper W, X, Y, or Z the best?"

The students engage in lively debate as they discuss the qualities of the papers they liked and why the other papers didn't make the mark. Eventually, students are ready to create a list of criteria for good writing which are posted in the classroom for easy reference. As Bonfils explains, "Its value as a guidepost for the students is that *they* wrote it."

What Makes Good Writing?
- *It makes sense.*
- *The events are clear.*
- *You can understand the words.*
- *It's neat enough to read.*
- *It's long because it had to be to tell a complete story.*
- *It's short; it told a lot in a little.*
- *It's interesting.*
- *It has details.*
- *Action words make it exciting.*
- *There may be spelling mistakes but we can figure them out.*

Inviting students to debate and determine standards of excellence is not only valuable but necessary. As teachers who want to make a real difference, we will want to nudge our students to achieve mutually-developed, rigorous standards for quality across the curriculum. When drawing a still life, for example, students might debate the value of line, shape, color, texture, or design. Or when engaged in a movement exercise, they might consider the qualities of space, shape, direction, size, or level. The more we can involve our students in thinking about and establishing the criteria for effective representations of all aspects of their learning, the more likely they will be to consciously strive to achieve those qualities in their own work.

What about scoring? Often, not only do we need to establish criteria for excellence and nudge our students toward achieving them, but we also need to score the final product. It is never easy to assign grades or numbers—particularly when we're having to judge a work of art. On the other hand, the scoring process can be immensely helpful, forcing us and our students to think through and articulate what we value.

Increasingly, schools are moving away from the five letter grades—A, B, C, D, and F—and working, instead, to establish rubrics, a numbered scale that spells out in some detail the value associated with each point on the scale. Want to try your hand at writing rubrics for your classroom? The California State Department of Education offers these suggestions:

- Think about what you would like to see and hear from students in each discipline—what would be ideal? Brainstorm a list of criteria.

- Include in your ideal not only the final product but also students' ability to write and talk about what they have learned. Can they use the vocabulary of a particular discipline? Can they tell why one thing is better than another? Can they relate specific details about what they have learned; for example, can they identify a particular dance or tell when a picture was painted?
- Write a description of this ideal achievement. To ensure that your ideal relates to the content standards set by your state or district, whenever possible, compare your description to existing curriculum guidelines.

The California State Department of Education recommends that you create a six-point scale because then you are forced to discriminate between the upper (4, 5, 6) and the lower (1, 2, 3). Generally, the upper half is viewed as "passing," while the lower half is deemed "unsatisfactory." If you were to work with an odd number of points, it might be too easy to settle on the middle score which wouldn't yield much information. Your ideal will be represented by the 6 on the six-point scale. Once you've established a description of a 6, write descriptions of the remaining five numbers. Whenever possible, I recommend that you create rubrics with your colleagues and students, and extend and refine your view of the ideal against theirs.

The rubric is not intended as a checklist of completed items, but as a guide to quality.

As you begin to use your rubric, try not to worry about whether you have students who achieve a level 6 or whether you maintain an even number of each level in your class. Ideally, the rubric will help you improve your students' learning. If none of your students achieve above a 3 or 4, then you'll want to examine factors that might be affecting their achievement such as the time you devote to the project, your availability, issues related to second language learning, students' previous knowledge, the money available for supplies and reference materials, and so on.

Keep in mind, as well, that the content standards you identify are targets you want your students to aim for. The rubric is not intended as a checklist of completed items, but as a guide to quality. Use your expert knowledge of each discipline together with the qualities you've identified in the rubric to assess your students' achievement.

To help us understand what a rubric is and how it might work, let's visit the classroom of elementary teacher Marla Tracy whose work in the arts is cited in the California State Department of Education's *Prelude to Performance Assessment in the Arts* (1993). Tracy teaches music at Junction Elementary School in Palo Cedro, California, where she engages her students in an in-depth study of flutes. First she helps them learn about the background of flutes and how to make them. Then they learn about myths and tone poems. They form groups, compose flute music for the myths, and, using their home-made flutes, perform their original music in groups.

Field Notes: Teacher-To-Teacher

Evaluation, as defined by Webster, means "to find the worth or value of, to appraise one's deed." I think of evaluation in the same way—to find the value of one's work. This applies not only to the student but to the teacher as well. I am convinced that we are our own best evaluators as we sit in judgment over our own products. Setting personal standards motivates us to work harder. Teachers and students together need to set standards if evaluation is to truly help us find the worth or value of one's own deeds.

Nancy Gates
Savannah Elementary School
Rosemead, California

To assess the quality of the final performance, Tracy and her students created a rubric. Then both she and her students used the rubric to evaluate each group's performance.

Level 6. A well-thought-out and organized presentation. All team members perform appropriate parts. The original story or myth is clearly narrated and well supported with the flute music, which is appropriate to the story. The cultural presentation is well explained, that is, techniques and musical customs are clearly presented. Costumes and props add to the presentation.

Level 5. Has all the required components, but is deficient in some details. For example, not all the members of the group play their homemade flutes.

Level 4. An adequate presentation that tells the story but is ragged and unpolished.

Level 3. A good attempt but deficient in clarity of narration or explanation, or lacking in musical quality.

Level 2. An attempt, but significantly lacking in musical execution.

Level 1. Minimal attempt, with little evidence of planning or interest in the presentation.

There are many ways to create and use rubrics, of course. Here's an example of a thirteen point rubric that a teacher shared with me during a conference, designed to be used over time as a way to assess students' ongoing involvement with literature, particularly in social studies and history.

Reader Response

Experiments with ideas	☐ Often	☐ Seldom	☐ Rarely
Fills in gaps	☐ Often	☐ Seldom	☐ Rarely
Deals with ambiguities	☐ Often	☐ Seldom	☐ Rarely
Deepens interpretations	☐ Often	☐ Seldom	☐ Rarely
Examines reader's prior knowledge with author's ideas	☐ Often	☐ Seldom	☐ Rarely
Challenges the text	☐ Often	☐ Seldom	☐ Rarely
Demonstrates understanding of the work as a whole	☐ Often	☐ Seldom	☐ Rarely
Shows how the parts work together	☐ Often	☐ Seldom	☐ Rarely
Shows aesthetic appreciation	☐ Often	☐ Seldom	☐ Rarely
Makes connections (own ideas, other literature, experiences)	☐ Often	☐ Seldom	☐ Rarely
Demonstrates emotional engagement	☐ Often	☐ Seldom	☐ Rarely
Retells	☐ Often	☐ Seldom	☐ Rarely
Reflects on universal significance of piece	☐ Often	☐ Seldom	☐ Rarely

S H O P T A L K

Wolf, Dennie Palmer and Nancy Pistone. *Taking Full Measure: Rethinking Assessment Through the Arts.* New York: College Entrance Examination Board, 1991.

This book focuses on five artistic disciplines—photography, theater, music, dance, and the visual arts—and examines a range of strategies teachers are using to encourage critical and thoughtful student analysis. Although each teacher in the book emphasizes discipline-specific skills, common threads of reflection, self-evaluation, and discussions of standards of excellence unite them. Readers will discover how the evaluation lessons learned in these arts classrooms can guide teaching and learning in all classrooms.

```
┌─────────────────────────────────────────────────────────────┐
│                      D I A L O G U E                          │
│                                                               │
│   How do I use rubrics?                                       │
│                                                               │
│   _____         │
│                                                               │
│   _____         │
│                                                               │
│   How do I establish the scale?                               │
│                                                               │
│   _____         │
│                                                               │
│   _____         │
│                                                               │
│   If you haven't tried writing a rubric, choose a discipline  │
│   you feel comfortable with and think about what would        │
│   represent the ideal response. If possible, compare your     │
│   ideal with that of your colleagues and state or district    │
│   curriculum guidelines.                                      │
│                                                               │
│   _____         │
│                                                               │
│   _____         │
│                                                               │
│   _____         │
│                                                               │
│   _____         │
│                                                               │
│   Once you've established the ideal, record it, and write out │
│   the remaining descriptions for each level. A six-point      │
│   scale works best.                                           │
└─────────────────────────────────────────────────────────────┘
```

5. Reporting: Summing Up

At some point, you need to organize the assessment data you've collected in meaningful ways so you can share it with parents, administrators, and others beyond the classroom door. As the ultimate goal of the evaluation process is self-evaluation for both students and teachers, it's best if your students are involved in the process every step of the way. Students should keep records of their own learning experiences and meet with you in conferences to evaluate what they have accomplished and what goals they hope to achieve—planning with you how these are to be met.

Nan Mohr, fifth-sixth grade teacher at Emma W. Shuey School in Rosemead, California, asks her students to complete the self-evaluation form on page 46 once they have completed a project from *Different Ways of Knowing*. She asks them to think about what they learned and how they learned it, including how they worked with their peers.

Self-Evaluation

Name _____ Date _____

I enjoyed working on this project.

     0   1   2   3   4   5   6   7   8   9   10

Not at all   Somewhat   A great deal

My effort on this project was

     0   1   2   3   4   5   6   7   8   9   10

Not as good   Above average   My best ever

as my usual   for me

In working on this project, I most enjoyed

☐ Working on my own   ☐ Working with a partner   ☐ Working in a group

The best thing about working on this project was _____

_____

The thing I liked least about working on this project was _____

_____

Some things I learned about history: _____

_____

_____

Some things I learned about oral presentation: _____

_____

_____

Each semester, using the "Reading Evaluation" form she developed on page 47, Debra Goodman, at the Dewey Learning Center in Detroit, evaluates each student as a reader on nine points. She also writes her major goal for each student, suggesting the ways in which the student might improve his or her reading ability. She then gives the forms to her students and asks them to respond to the same points as well as to her evaluation. Next, the evaluation is sent home so that parents may read Goodman's evaluation of their child and the child's response to the evaluation. Parents are asked to respond to both. In this way, Goodman establishes a close partnership with both students and parents.

Reading Evaluation

Name Renata

Date 1-91

	Teacher Comment	Student Comment	Parent Comment
Selects books to read	Reading Black Beauty	I have an long book to read.	Treat book
Reads independently	Renata is beginning to read for longer time periods	I like to read some time	Some time
Reads at home	Please turn in reading homework each week.	I am reading at home	Forget reading sheet
Enjoys reading	yes	I Like to read.	yes
Understands what he/she reads	Yes. Renata reflects a good understanding	I understand how to read some h read books	yes
Reads a variety of materials	Enjoys stories and novels	I read storyes	yes
Enjoys listening to stories	Sometimes	I listen in some times.	Sometimes
Reflects on reading in discussion	Renata often participates	I tell about my books	Great job!
Reflects upon reading in writing	Renata does a good job in her reading	my best book that I raed blakbeauty	? her spelling

Major goal for semester

Teacher I would like to see Renata read for at least 20 minutes every day.

Student I want to raed for 30 minents

Parent Renata has improved w/ reading skill during homework hours.

                        Thank You
            Mrs Janice Grant

DIALOGUE

Most teachers agree that parents are our most valuable teaching partners. But finding ways to pull parents in and make them feel an integral part of the evaluation process is more difficult.

How do I keep parents apprised of their children's progress? Through conferences? letters? phone calls?

_____

How do I involve parents in evaluating their children's work?

_____

What might I do to increase parent involvement?

_____

In sum, every learning experience is an opportunity for assessment. As you continuously evaluate and monitor your students' learning through record keeping, observing, interacting, and analyzing learning artifacts, you can design instruction and create curriculum that will stretch your students' knowledge and expand their worlds.

SHOPTALK

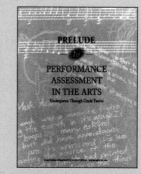

California State Department of Education. *Prelude to Performance Assessment in the Arts.* Sacramento: California State Department of Education, 1993.

From the California State Department of Education, which has been at the forefront of American educational reform, comes this booklet, the beginning of an exciting dialogue on assessment in the arts. Teachers of dance, drama and theater, music, and the visual arts share the strategies and techniques they've developed through the state-sponsored Towards Arts Assessment Project (TAAP). The result is an inspiring and informative pamphlet on ways to assess students' artistic endeavors, increase teacher and student learning, and bring deeper meaning to all arts experiences in classrooms, K-12.

Chapter 3

Assessment Tools for Learning and Teaching

We need to find new ways and new tools that will provide as many windows as possible into the subtle complexities of the mind. Our goal as evaluators and teachers is to document, as richly as possible, our students' learning and to accomplish this in a deeply thoughtful manner. To that end, we need to use an array of assessment tools from a variety of perspectives. This chapter presents a sampling of such tools from each one of the five kidwatching perspectives described in Chapter 2. I've included some sample forms. Adapt the forms to meet your own needs and interests.

1. Monitoring: Keeping Track

Once upon a time, keeping track was relatively easy. Kids sat apart in rows. They stayed in their seats and did their work. All children had the same stack of work and were expected to complete it at the same time. Keeping track was as simple as marking off the assigned textbook pages.

Keeping track is not as simple in learner-centered classrooms. Children work collaboratively, often on projects of their own choosing. Not everyone is doing the same thing at the same time. New instructional strategies demand new ways of keeping track.

But the burden of monitoring shouldn't fall solely on your shoulders. As with all aspects of assessment, students should take the lead in keeping track and documenting their own learning experiences.

New instructional strategies demand new ways of keeping track.

Field Notes: Teacher-To-Teacher

My students participate in a variety of evaluative activities. They complete reading evaluations, answer questions about the material they enjoy reading and about the processes they use to figure out unfamiliar words. Students complete reflection sheets which help them explore what they have learned from various assignments. They evaluate their writing processes and final drafts, and build portfolios. Students share these portfolios with their families, who are invited to share their responses.

Deborah Ventura
Jane Addams Elementary School
Lawndale, California

Tracking sheet. If your classroom is organized around learning centers, you may want to develop a tracking sheet. These help both you and your students keep track of the centers, the learning experiences the students have tried at the centers, their evaluations of their experiences, and what they might try next. In this way, although you can't observe every child at work in every center, you can check their tracking sheets, and, at a glance, discover what they've tried, how it went, and what they should do next.

My Center Tracking Sheet

Name _____

Week of _____

Centers	Date Started	Date Completed	Self-Evaluation

The most effective learners are often those who can direct, monitor, and document their own learning. Elementary teacher Debra Goodman has developed "My Plans" for her students, shown on page 52, which lists each week's activities—those that are required as well as those that are optional. She requires her students to check the form as they complete each activity. In this way, her students understand their options and feel choice and ownership over their own learning.

At learner-centered Lowell Elementary School in Missoula, Montana, students must meet weekly requirements, but how and when they choose to complete their assignments is up to them. In addition, they are free to choose from a variety of center activities. To help them and their teachers monitor their choices and progress, they complete the "Weekly Schedule" on page 53, developed by a group of Lowell teachers, in which they identify and evaluate their work choices. The schedule is handed in at the end of the week with a folder of the week's work. Teachers review the folders and the schedules, and they use the comments box to respond.

Both of these forms, My Plans and the Weekly Schedule, reflect the curriculum and instructional programs of the teachers who created them. If these forms look useful to you, you can adapt them in ways that fit your curriculum and classroom.

Field Notes: Teacher-To-Teacher

A certain amount of trust is necessary as students record their own work. Learning to keep good records takes time. Initially, I take some class time to have students fill out their My Plans record sheets following time spent in centers, reading, writing, and so on. As students learn to work independently and record their own work, I can review record sheets quickly and pull those that look spotty. While I don't equate learning with good records, I do push students to keep good records of their learning experiences. Their ongoing self-evaluation helps them learn to recognize and share with others their own strengths, abilities, and achievements. Students can see the immediate value of the process, since it enables them to get credit for a variety of learning experiences, both at school and at home.

Debra Goodman
Dewey Learning Center
Detroit, Michigan

My Plans

Name _____ Week of _____

1. Quiet Work Center (Research)

_____ a. Listen to a story or author tape   _____ d. Wherezit (a geography game)

_____ b. Work on your portfolio   _____ e. Jigsaw puzzle

_____ c. Map activity or map puzzle   _____ f. Research: your choice

2. Post Office/Writing Center

_____ a. Write a letter   _____ c. Writing: your choice

_____ b. Write with a story starter

3. Library

_____ a. Choose a book to read   _____ d. Meet with your literature group

_____ b. Write with a story starter   _____ e. Reading: your choice

_____ c. Work on a reading response

4. Science Center

_____ a. Make an observation of your plant   _____ d. Write or draw about a science topic

_____ b. Science activity (with activity sheet)   _____ e. Science: your choice

_____ c. Read a science book or magazine

5. Math Center

_____ a. Meet with your math group   _____ e. Geoboard worksheet

_____ b. Fraction bars game (record your results) _____ f. Cuisenaire rods activity

_____ c. Design block activity   _____ g. Math: your choice

_____ d. Math puzzler

6. Work Center

_____ a. Writing   _____ e. Journal

_____ b. Reading response   _____ f. Science

_____ c. Math   _____ g. Work: your choice

_____ d. Ranger Rick's

7. Free Choice (completed two work choices for day)

_____ a. Draw   _____ e. Knitting

_____ b. Chess   _____ f. Book illustration

_____ c. Legos   _____ g. Your choice

_____ d. Checkers

	Monday	Tuesday	Wednesday	Thursday	Friday
Reading	_____	_____	_____	_____	_____
Journal	_____	_____	_____	_____	_____
Work 1	_____	_____	_____	_____	_____

The Whole Language Catalog: Forms for Authentic Assessment © 1994 edited by Lois Bridges Bird, Kenneth S. Goodman and Yetta M. Goodman

Weekly Schedule

Name_____ Date _____

Literature: Title _____ Author _____

        Read from _____ to _____ by _____

Handwriting _____

_____

Art _____

_____

Homework _____

_____

Research _____

_____

Math _____

_____

Social Science _____

_____

Spelling: (Write words in personal dictionary)_____

_____

Silent Reading: Title _____ Author _____

_____

Creative Writing _____

_____

Science _____

_____

Center Activities _____

_____

Other Reading_____

_____

I learned _____

_____

Comments _____

_____

_____

Status of the class. Middle school teacher Nancie Atwell (1987) found that a quick check-in with each student at the start of the school day is important in helping her and her students keep track of who is doing what. The procedure is straightforward and simple. Before class, the kids gather on a rug in a circle with Atwell. In three minutes, Atwell goes around the circle and asks each student to state what he or she plans to work on that morning. Using a code she has developed, she marks a grid containing every student's name. Atwell uses this system to keep track of her writing workshop.

Maureen White, the K-8 writing coordinator for Haverhill School District in Haverhill, Massachusetts, created her own version of the "Status of the Class" checksheet to help her keep track of the writing workshops she conducts. You can adapt the form to keep track of any aspect of your curriculum.

Writing Workshop: Status of the Class

Name_____   Grade _____

Legend: 1. New text   2. Conferencing   3. Revising
           4. Working on draft   5. Computing   6. Editing

Names _____

1. _____
2. _____
3. _____
4. _____
5. _____
6. _____
7. _____
8. _____

The Whole Language Catalog: Forms for Authentic Assessment © 1994 edited by Lois Bridges Bird, Kenneth S. Goodman and Yetta M. Goodman

Contracts. A contract can work in much the same way as a planning or tracking sheet. As the name suggests, a contract is a written agreement between the student and teacher, and sometimes parents, in which the activities the child will complete for the day or week are listed. The contract may address the daily required work or special projects children will work on in their free time. The students read their contract—or design it for themselves—and then they sign it, agreeing to the contract's terms. The teacher signs it, too, and may send it home for parents to sign. In this way, all partners are informed of and agree to the expectations for learning.

One primary class anticipating their involvement in independent research projects, designed their own research contract, shown on the next page, complete with signature lines for witnesses.

Research Contract
Developed by a third-grade class

I, _____, am anxious to do research on

(topic, ideas) _____

My plan of study will be _____

_____

I will use the following resources: _____

_____

The date I will start is _____

I will present a progress report on _____

and conclude my study on_____

I shall present my activity in the form of

☐ class presentation   ☐ report
☐ play   ☐ other _____

I understand that I am able to negotiate a new contract at the time of my progress report if need be.

_____   _____
Signed   Date

_____   _____
Witness   Date

Simple lists are another easy yet effective way for students to monitor and keep track of their learning experiences. What should they list?

- Books they've read. They might include the date they started and finished the book, the author's name, the number of pages, and their thoughts and feelings about the book. If you assign homework, consider asking parents and children to spend twenty minutes reading together nightly. You might send a simple form home encouraging them to keep a record of the books they've shared together. An example is shown on the following page.
- Written compositions they've published. They could include the date they started and finished, writing conventions they tried and feel they now control, and comments from those who have read the published work. The "Writing Workshop Record" on page 57, developed by a classroom teacher, was shared with me at a teacher's conference and serves as a good example.

Home and School Independent Reading

Name_____   Grade _____

Title of Book and Author	Date Started	Date Finished	Genre of Book	Comments

The Whole Language Catalog: Forms for Authentic Assessment © 1994 edited by Lois Bridges Bird, Kenneth S. Goodman and Yetta M. Goodman

Writing Workshop Record		

Name_____ Date _____ Grade _____ Quarter _____

Date	What I Worked On	Notes

2. Observing: What's Going On?

Considering the busy, fast-paced nature of classrooms, teachers are remarkably adept at intuitively following what every student is doing. Still, written records of classroom observations are most helpful. Besides enabling you to preserve specific learning events for each child, written records provide guidelines for observing: What sort of information should you observe? How should you record the data? How does one interpret it? How might it be shared?

The key to successful kidwatching is to find a system that works for you. Some teachers prefer anecdotal forms. Others like keeping a loose-leaf notebook with a section for each child; others write on mailing labels that they peel off and place inside a manila folder for each child. Experiment and discover the system you think is both manageable and worthwhile.

Mailing labels and anecdotal observation form. Primary teacher Katherine Der Mugrdechian, who teaches at Burroughs Elementary School in Fresno, California, records her kidwatching data on mailing labels and stores them on a form she developed herself. Der Mugrdechian explains:

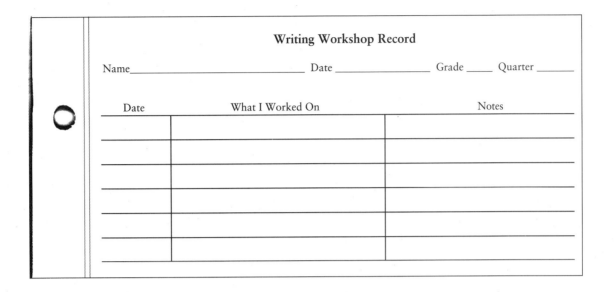

> My students have an Anecdotal Record Sheet that is stored in their language arts folders. The sheet is divided into six areas: reading, writing, math, oral language, inside play, outside play. These can be changed to other focuses in other years or I can

add other focuses on the reverse side. Using copier labels (or address labels for dry-toner office copiers), I type the names in the master spacer and run the copier label sheets in place of paper. Each child's name is on one sheet (each sheet has thirty-two labels). With the sheet of labels on a clipboard, it becomes very easy to target an area for observation and write down my comments for each child, as well as to know which children remain to be observed. Once all the children have been observed for a specific area, I date the labels and place them in the corresponding space on the Anecdotal Record Sheet in their language arts folders.

Anecdotal Record

Name _____ Date_____ Grade_____

Reading _____

Writing _____

Math _____

Oral Language _____

Inside Play _____

Outside Play _____

The Whole Language Catalog: Forms for Authentic Assessment © 1994 edited by Lois Bridges Bird, Kenneth S. Goodman and Yetta M. Goodman

Anecdotal record sheets provide a holistic view of the children and what they have done throughout the year.

Primary teachers Diana Mazzuchi, Nancy Brooks, and Maggi Shine, who teach a multiage class in Brattleboro, Vermont, also use an anecdotal form to record their kidwatching. Their focus is on four learning strategies across the curriculum—question posing, risk-taking, collaboration and cooperation, and sharing knowledge.

In a similar way, Penny Silvers (1994), a K-3 coordinator in Prichett School, Buffalo Grove, Illinois, uses an anecdotal form that centers on learning strategies embedded in four different learning contexts—whole group, small group, individual, and other. When she records her observations, she notes

Anecdotal Observations

Student _____ Date_____ Grade_____

Learning Contexts	Strategies	Risk-Taking	Collaboration	Inquiry	Reflection

"Everyday Signs of Learning: Inquiry-Based Evaluation," *Primary Voices K-6* © 1994 by Penny Silvers

under Learning Contexts whether children are working alone, in small groups, with the whole class, or in other learning arrangements.

The Primary Language Record. The PLR is perhaps the most detailed and widely used anecdotal record-keeping system. Developed in Great Britain by leading language educators headed by Myra Barr, it evaluates student progress in the language arts.

The PLR includes interviews with students and parents, and recommendations for instruction that teachers, students, and parents do together. Particularly helpful are the observation forms of language across the curriculum: listening, speaking, reading, and writing. Teachers are asked to record information about their students' developing language in a variety of social and instructional contexts three times a year. The PLR provides teachers with detailed theoretical information about language and learning, explains what sort of information to record, how to record and interpret it, and how to develop instructional and curriculum strategies to extend and refine their students' understanding. The *Primary Language Record*, including the observational forms, is published in the U.S. by Heinemann.

S H O P T A L K

Barr, Mary. *California Learning Record: Handbook for Teachers K-6.* Sacramento: California State Department of Education, 1994.

The *California Learning Record* is an excellent adaptation of the *Primary Language Record.* Mary Barr, the director of the CLR, has also developed a math observation form; she and her team plan to extend the CLR across the curriculum.

Taking time out to observe one child at work—never mind thirty-plus students—may seem like a daunting, if not an impossible extra task for a busy teacher. But since the most effective teaching stems from really knowing and understanding our students, kidwatching is not an extra task—it's a a necessary one. To make it manageable as well, Palo Alto School District in Palo Alto, California, developed these kidwatching guidelines for its teachers. Follow or adapt the guidelines. Find the approach that works for you.

Kidwatching Strategies

Below are some suggestions to help make kidwatching practical. This is not an exhaustive or definitive list, but it is meant to help you get started.

Fitting Everyone In

- Choose one student per day to observe. Follow him or her through an entire work period or even an entire day, noting areas of difficulty or success, learning strategies, interactions with others, and so on.
   - Divide your class into groups to observe a small number of students. This arrangement allows you to observe all students in a systematic, rotating fashion. For example, in a class of 30 children, you could watch three children every day and observe your whole class in 10 school days, or you could fit everyone into one week by observing six children a day.

- Choose children to observe with a particular purpose in mind. For example, a child not engaged in books may be having trouble choosing appropriate reading material. You could observe his or her selection process.
- Focus on a particular skill, behavior, or attitude. For example, you could observe your entire class in one work period by walking around and noting whether each child paragraphs as he or she writes.
- Note anything of particular interest as it happens. You may want to write down the first time a student volunteers to read aloud in front of others.

Freeing Yourself Up
- Observe while children are working independently.
- When students are working without needing a lot of direction or assistance, you can take this time to observe.
- Observe when there is another adult present.
- Observe during your release time. When someone else is teaching your class, you have an excellent opportunity to observe. It also may be interesting to note how your children behave and perform with another instructor.
- With another adult (i.e., parent, aide, student teacher) available to answer questions and offer help, it's often easier for you to free yourself up to observe.
- Observe when you have alerted students that you will be doing so. You can tell students you will be observing (and thus are unavailable to them except for emergencies) by announcing you are "invisible," putting up a sign such as "Teacher Is Out."
- Observe during a specified time. By setting aside a certain time to observe, your students will learn when you are available to them and when you are "invisible" because you are observing.

Since the most effective teaching stems from really knowing and understanding our students, kidwatching is not an extra task—it's a necessary one.

Keeping Track
- Self-stick notes—Write on self-stick notes, stick them into a manila folder, then transfer them onto an index card or into a notebook.
- Binder paper—Take notes on a clipboard and transfer them to a binder.
- Spiral notebook or composition book—Write directly into a notebook or copy notes from self-stick notes or binder paper. You can either keep running notes for the entire class, or have certain pages set apart for each student.

- Labels—Carry labels on a clipboard. As you observe a student, take short notes on a label. Write the date and the student's initials on the side and stick the label inside a manila folder to achieve a chronological account of your observations of each student.
- Index cards—Develop a file of index cards containing notes on each student. Carry index cards on a clipboard if you are observing particular students, or transfer notes onto the index cards.
- Checklist—At the top of a class list, note the particular skill, behavior, or ability you wish to observe. As you observe the students, check them off or make short notes to the side of their names. Keep the checklists in a notebook containing notes about the entire class. You can transfer particularly interesting information from the checklists to labels or index cards.

Checklists. Sometimes the process of developing a checklist is more valuable than actually using the checklist. As Ken Goodman (1992) suggests, the checklist is like the shopping list we carefully construct then leave at home when we go out to do our shopping. "The checklist serves the purpose of helping us to think through what our goals and priorities are and puts us in a frame of mind to be effective kidwatchers."

Constructing an observational checklist with your colleagues can lead to helpful dialogue regarding what information is significant, what should serve as developmental benchmarks, how the information will be gathered and collated, and what will be done with it after its collected and recorded. A cautionary note: keep the checklist simple. Long, complicated lists often end up in file drawers, unused.

Caryl Crowell, a bilingual teacher at Borton Primary Magnet School in Tucson, Arizona, developed the "Whole Language Checklist" shown on the next three pages. It's appropriate for primary through middle school students with some adaptation. She writes, "As I expanded my professional knowledge about evaluation and the development of literacy in children, my list began to reflect not only the behaviors I observed in my students, but the ones I hoped to see. In other words, the list was a statement of my goals for the class as well as a record of what was already occurring. I update it continually and send it home quarterly to enable parents to see how their child's literacy is developing. I deliberately leave lots of room for comments on the checklist and encourage parents to make use of this space to let me know about important literacy events at home."

Whole Language Checklist

Name _____ Date _____ Grade _____

Native language _____ Second language _____

Evaluation code: 1-rarely   3-often
                   2-sometimes   4-always

Oral Language Development	1	2	3	4	Comments
Listens attentively when others speak in one-to-one interactions					
in small groups					
in large groups					
to stories read aloud					
Participates and takes turns appropriately in conversations					
Elaborates responses					
Explains thinking					
Talks about language					
Engages in language play					
Demonstrates understanding of oral directions					
Literacy Development–Reading					
Selects own reading material					
Initiates reading promptly					
Reads for a sustained period					
Reads a variety of material					
Reads for enjoyment, information, and research					
Attempts to make meaningful substitutions for unknown words					
Uses language sense and meaning to make and confirm predictions					
Monitors own reading and self-corrects					
Literacy Development–Literature Response					
Retells and summarizes stories					
Relates reading to personal experiences					
Demonstrates awareness of story elements: plot, characters, theme, setting					
Recognizes a variety of genre: fairy tale, folktale, poetry, drama, biography					
Discusses reading with others					
Extends reading experiences through other related reading and projects					
Writes thoughtfully in literature log					

Writing	1	2	3	4	Comments
Self-selects writing topics and ideas					
Engages promptly in and sustains writing activities					
Writes for a variety of purposes and audiences					
Uses a variety of styles, forms, and literary devices					
Ideas/stories are developed cohesively and sequentially					
Writing shows character and theme development					
Uses a variety of vocabulary and sentence structures					
Writes in paragraphs with topic sentences and supporting details					
Shares and discusses writing with others for clarity and meaning					
Self-edits for conventions					
Uses appropriate resources to support writing process					
Writing Mechanics					
Explores uses of punctuation					
Uses end punctuation appropriately					
Uses other punctuation appropriately					
Uses capitals and lower case letters appropriately					
Uses age-appropriate handwriting					
Spelling					
Uses invented spelling freely					
Invented spellings are easily read and show appropriate letter-sound correspondences					
High frequency words show standard spelling					
Invented spelling shows awareness of spelling patterns					
Spelling shows visualization of words					
Many words show standard spelling					
Math Problem Solving					
Uses manipulatives effectively					
Uses representational drawings appropriately					
Solves problems at the abstract level					
Attempts to solve problems in an organized way					

	1	2	3	4	Comments
Estimates answers					
Considers reasonableness of answers					
Discusses problem-solving strategies					
Keeps working when answer is not immediately apparent					
Makes mental calculations					
Learning in a Social Environment					
Is organized and has necessary materials					
Begins work promptly and stays on task to appropriate closure or completion					
Self-directed and self-motivated					
Uses room resources for information and clarification					
Uses other children as resources					
Collaborates effectively with others; does his or her share					
Values ideas and contributions of others					
Interactions show respect for safety and feelings of others					
Assumes responsibility for solving social problems verbally					
Takes risks as a learner					
Self-evaluates					
Second Language Development					
Demonstrates interest in learning a second language					
Listens attentively when second language is used					
Attempts purposeful communication in second language					
Builds/draws upon knowledge of native language					
Demonstrates ongoing development of literacy in second language					

General Comments (to be used by parents and teacher)

The Whole Language Catalog: Forms for Authentic Assessment © 1994 edited by Lois Bridges Bird, Kenneth S. Goodman and Yetta M. Goodman

```
DIALOGUE

Have I tried keeping anecdotal records of my classroom observa-
tions? If so, how do I structure and organize my observations?

_____

_____


How do I record them?

_____


Does my system work? Why or why not? What changes could I
make?

_____

_____


How do I use the data I record? Do I share it with parents and stu-
dents? How?

_____

_____
```

Sometimes we forget that the easiest way to understand what our students are thinking is to simply ask.

3. Interacting: Finding Out

I've heard Frank Smith tell the story about a young teacher who approached him and explained that she was dying to find out what one student, who was something of a puzzle to her, thought about her class and curriculum. "How can I find out what he is thinking, Professor Smith?" Smith answered her with his own question, "Have you asked him?"

Sometimes, in our desire to "see inside our students' heads," we forget that the easiest way in may be through simple conversation—to simply ask the student what he or she is thinking. Questions we might ask include: "What steps did you follow as you solved this long division problem? Tell me about your spelling of elephant. How did you decide to represent your social studies research as a dance?" Our students often have ready answers. We need only ask, and they will respond with valuable insights into their own learning.

In addition to asking questions that nudge our students to think beyond their current patterns of knowing, we can also engage them in more formal interviews, even tape recording the session for later transcription or analysis.

Burke Reading Interview. Would you like to uncover your students' thinking about their own reading strategies? Try the Burke Reading Interview. Developed by Carolyn Burke of the University of Indiana (1987), it encourages students to turn thought in on language (metalinguistic awareness) and consider their attitudes toward and feelings about themselves as readers.

This interview should be conducted in an informal setting, relatively free of interruption. Notations of the student's responses can be made in an anecdotal record or in other suitable form.

1. When you are reading and you come to something you don't know, what do you do? Do you ever do anything else?
2. Do you think that (teacher's name) is a good reader? Who is a good reader you know?
3. What makes him or her a good reader?
4. Do you think that good readers ever come to something they don't know when they are reading?
5. If yes: When they come to something they don't know, what do you think they do about it?
6. If you know that someone was having difficulty reading, how would you help?
7. What would your teacher do to help that person?
8. How did you learn to read? Who or what helped you learn?
9. What would you like to do better as a reader?
10. Do you think you are a good reader?

You can easily adapt the Burke Reading Interview to gain insight into students' self-awareness in other curriculum areas. For example, W. Rex Comer, a dance specialist for the Galef Institute, adapted the interview to tap into his students' thoughts and feelings regarding dance.

- What do you think dance is?
- What do people do when they dance?
- Do you ever dance? When?
- Who is a good dancer you know?
- What makes a person a good dancer?
- Do you know how to dance?
- What do you do when you dance?
- How did you learn to dance?
- Do you like to dance?
- Do you think you are a good dancer? Why?
- What kinds of dance do you do?

- Do you ever watch other people dance? What kind? Where? Why?
- How often do you dance?
- Did you dance when you were younger? When? Where? How?
- Do you think you will dance when you are older?
- Do you like to dance for others? When?
- What would you like to learn about dance?

Conferences. The following peer conferencing guidelines created by Lucy Calkins for those teachers involved with writing process are equally adaptable. At the beginning of the school year, Maureen White, the writing coordinator for Haverhill School District in Haverhill, Massachusetts, models the peer

Peer Conferencing Guidelines

Speak in quiet voices during peer conferencing. Other writers may be drafting, and it's hard to think when your thoughts are interrupted. Support each other by sharing your strategies.

Writer	Listener
Share your work with another writer. Each person reads his or her own piece to the listener. You may want to ask the listener for help on a particular aspect of the piece, such as "Let me know if I've been less wordy this time."	**Look and listen to the writer who is sharing.** The listener should listen carefully and take notes so that she or he can point out places where the writing worked well. You may ask the writer to repeat a part, read more slowly, loudly, and so on.
Listen carefully to the comments of the listener. You may take notes on the suggestions and later consider using them.	**Tell the writer what you heard.** Tell the writer a detail you liked about the text. Use specific details, such as "I enjoyed the description of your school's locker room as 'pungent with the odor of old sweat socks'."
Decide how or if to use the conferencing suggestions. Remember, the purpose of conferencing is to lead the writer directly to revising (adding, deleting, changing) her or his text.	**Say to the writer, "Tell me more about…"** or "What do you mean by…" or "I'm confused by…" Feel free to ask the writer any questions about her or his piece.
	Avoid telling the author what to do with her or his piece. Avoid the words "You should." Remember not to take away the writer's ownership.

The Whole Language Catalog: Forms for Authentic Assessment © 1994 edited by Lois Bridges Bird, Kenneth S. Goodman and Yetta M. Goodman

conferencing guidelines for her young writers and then invites them to use them to obtain peer feedback on their writing. You can adapt the guidelines so that students can use them to give feedback on a classmate's dance, dramatic presentation, visual sketch, or musical composition.

Interest inventories. Interest inventories, questionnaires, or interviews that reveal students' interests can be very helpful, particularly at the beginning of the school year when our primary concern is getting to know our students. If it seems overwhelming to interview each student, ask older students to read the inventory and write the answers in themselves. For younger students, invite parents in to help. Older peer tutors can also help interview young students and record their answers.

Les Persson, an elementary teacher at Windmill Springs School in San Jose, California, has fully embraced Howard Gardner's theory of multiple intelligences. Persson strives to expand the literacy spectrum in his classroom and offers multiple entries into his curriculum—spatial, bodily-kinesthetic, interpersonal, intrapersonal, and musical, as well as the more traditional linguistic and logical-mathematical. In this way, Persson finds, all children can succeed. At the beginning of the year, he administers his adaptations of the "Checklist for Assessing Students' Multiple Intelligences" from *Multiple Intelligences in the Classroom* by Thomas Armstrong. Persson interviews students himself or has parents complete the form to discover early on how individual students learn most effectively. Some of Persson's questions include:

- Does your child like to write stories? (linguistic intelligence)
- Does your child ask questions about how things work? (logical-mathematical intelligence)
- Does your child easily read diagrams and maps? (spatial intelligence)
- Does your child like to take objects apart and put them back together again? (bodily-kinesthetic intelligence)
- Does your child play a musical instrument? (musical intelligence)
- Does your child take charge in a group setting? (interpersonal intelligence)
- Does your child have a good sense of his or her own moods or behaviors? (intrapersonal intelligence)

SHOPTALK

Armstrong, Thomas. *Multiple Intelligences in the Classroom.* Alexandria, Virginia: Association for Supervision and Curriculum Development, 1994.

Armstrong effectively brings the theory of multiple intelligences and the reality of classroom practice together. In clear, readable language, Armstrong explains the underpinnings of multiple intelligences theory. He emphasizes that everyone possesses all seven intelligences and that, while we may be naturally stronger in some areas, each can be developed. Armstrong gives specific teaching strategies for each intelligence, for example he suggests integrating kinesthetic activities like the game charades into the curriculum by having students pantomime concepts from soil erosion to supply and demand. Other areas of the book discuss applying a multiple intelligences perspective to curriculum development, classroom environment, and assessment, including portfolio building. Armstrong includes a Checklist for Assessing Students' Multiple Intelligences and an MI Inventory for Adults, both of which are useful in identifying personal strengths. Helpful appendices include annotated reading lists on MI theory and teaching with multiple intelligences, along with examples of MI lessons and programs, K-12.

Parent-student-teacher questionnaires. Communicating with parents is an important aspect of all effective learner-centered classrooms. Parents should understand the philosophy underlying your program, the curriculum as it is translated into classroom practice, and the ways in which you plan to evaluate your students' progress. And it helps immeasurably as a teacher if you understand your students, their home experiences, and parents' expectations for their education. Frequent communication with parents supports home-school dialogue.

Cathy Howard at Ohlone School in Palo Alto, California, initiates a dialogue with her parents by sending home the following questionnaire the first week of school. "Getting To Know Your Child" helps Howard understand her primary students and their home experiences. She also learns about parents' expectations for their children's education. Her letter and questionnaire helps establish an educational partnership that lasts throughout the year.

Getting To Know Your Child

Dear Parents:

This information is most helpful to me as I get to know your child and you. Please send it at your earliest convenience. Thank you.

- *What changes (health, maturity, interests) have occurred in the life of your child this summer?*
- *What areas of school life has your child especially enjoyed?*
- *Toward what areas of school life has your child expressed negative or ambivalent feelings?*
- *In general, how is your child's self-concept? Does your child believe in his or her abilities?*
- *What special needs (academic, social, personal) does your child have?*
- *What goals do you have for your child this year?*
- *Where does your child go after school?*
- *What are favorite after-school or weekend interests and activities?*
- *What else do you want me to know about your child or about you?*

From _____ Date_____

D I A L O G U E

By asking just the right question at the right moment, we can nudge students into new realms of knowing. You may discover that certain types of questions invite children to examine their own thinking such as Do you think so? Is it possible? What might happen if...?

To begin developing the art of questioning, try keeping track of the questions you ask—of the whole class, small groups, and individual students.

_____

_____

_____

Note students' responses to your questions. Do your questions spark new questions? lead to independent research? result in stirring debate? Do the questions help students make connections to their own experiences, literature they are reading, and other curriculum units?

_____

_____

_____

_____

---

4. Analyzing Artifacts: Delving Deeper

The fourth kidwatching perspective centers on collecting and analyzing in greater depth the artifacts of learning: written stories and reports, sketches and drawings, videotapes of students' presentations, and so forth. These provide students, parents, teachers, and administrators with concrete evidence of progress. Also, involving students in the process of establishing the criteria for evaluation helps them understand what qualities count and what qualities to strive for in their own work. In fact, you may want to post the criteria in your classroom and refer to and discuss them frequently. Two ways you and your students might evaluate the artifacts of students' learning are through presentations and reading profiles.

Field Notes: Teacher-To-Teacher

I have begun to teach my students about reflection. Reflection is a form of evaluation. I really feel this is an important tool for them to learn. Too often they spend a great deal of time trying to figure out what their teacher wants and trying to please me. I am amazed at what they write to me in their reflective letters. They know if they spend time on an assignment and try their best, they usually do a good job. They also know that when they don't try, their response to the assignment is poor.

Carol Mahoney
Muscatel Middle School
Rosemead, California

Looking at a presentation. After students have participated in a learning experience, invite them to share with others what they have learned. And, in keeping with the theory of multiple intelligences, give students multiple ways to express themselves—through language, visual and performing arts, mathematic symbols, and personal interactions. When they share their learning, regardless of the format they choose in which to present it, here are some questions to consider:

- Is the information presented in a logical manner? Can the audience follow the student's line of thought?

- Is the piece saying one dominant thing? Does every element support and advance the main point?

- Voice allows the audience to hear an individual voice speaking from a piece. Is it engaging? Does it hold the audience's attention?

- Audiences crave specifics. Does the presenter include a depth and breadth of information: quotations, facts, statistics, concrete details, observations, anecdotes, and images?

- What was the student attempting to do? Does the student succeed?

At Ohlone School in Palo Alto, California, June Fuji immerses her nine- and ten-year-old students in a variety of hands-on projects. They simulate the lives of Coastal Miwuk Indians; they engage in an in-depth study of John Muir, spending the day at his former home experiencing what life was like more than 100 years ago; and they conduct independent research on topics of their own choosing related to colonial America. During all phases of student work, Fuji invites her students to present their learning to their peers. To help her students improve their presentational skills, she asks the audience to evaluate each presentation using this presentation feedback form.

Presentation Feedback

Presented by _____ Date _____

Subject _____

List three ideas you heard presented.

_____

_____

_____

Did the presenter:	All the time	Most of the time	Needs to practice
Have materials organized	_____	_____	_____
Speak clearly	_____	_____	_____
Maintain eye contact with the audience	_____	_____	_____
Avoid "umms" and "ahhs"	_____	_____	_____

Give the presenter one suggestion you feel would be helpful in future presentations.

_____

Tell the presenter what you liked best about this presentation._____

_____

Evaluator's name _____

Developing a reading profile. Becoming a reader is a complex, subtle process. In order to discover how your students are developing as readers, you'll want to explore a variety of data—their written responses to what they are reading, their talk about books and authors, retellings of stories they've read, awareness of their own reading strategies, and the like. As elementary teacher Debra Goodman reads through her nine- and ten-year-old students' reading logs, she uses "Developing a Reading Profile" to create a reading portrait of each student. As you read through the questions, you might consider how you can adapt them to apply to other content areas.

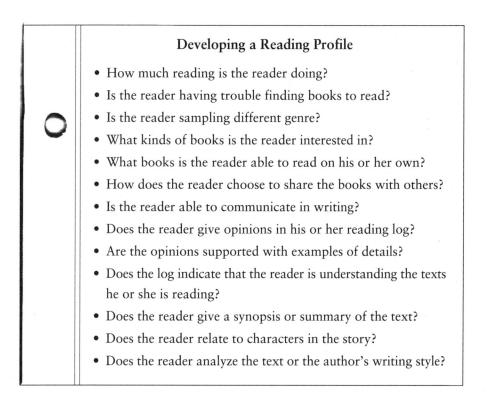

Developing a Reading Profile

- How much reading is the reader doing?
- Is the reader having trouble finding books to read?
- Is the reader sampling different genre?
- What kinds of books is the reader interested in?
- What books is the reader able to read on his or her own?
- How does the reader choose to share the books with others?
- Is the reader able to communicate in writing?
- Does the reader give opinions in his or her reading log?
- Are the opinions supported with examples of details?
- Does the log indicate that the reader is understanding the texts he or she is reading?
- Does the reader give a synopsis or summary of the text?
- Does the reader relate to characters in the story?
- Does the reader analyze the text or the author's writing style?

5. Reporting: Summing Up

Throughout the evaluation process, you'll want to organize in meaningful ways the assessment data you've collected so that you can share it with parents, administrators, and others. As the ultimate goal of an evaluation process is self-evaluation for both students and teachers, it's best if students are involved in the process every step of the way. Students can keep records of their own learning experiences and meet with you in conferences to evaluate what they have accomplished and what goals they hope to achieve, planning with you how these are to be met.

DIALOGUE

A reading profile can be changed to reflect other dimensions of the curriculum. Think of the kinds of questions you could use as a base to create a profile of a child as a visual artist, a mathematician, or a historian.

_____

_____

_____

_____

Chapter 4 explores in detail learning portfolios, one of the most effective ways to encourage student self-reflection and evaluation. However, there are numerous ways to encourage students to step outside of their learning experiences and engage in self-reflection. Here are some of my favorites.

Self-evaluation forms. Often we're unsure of the boundaries of a new learning territory until we've had a moment to stroll leisurely around the grounds. Time out for reflection is like a refreshing walk. It's an opportunity to escape the hustle-bustle of our active learning lives, and listen to ourselves think about what we've learned. Teacher or student-created self-evaluation forms help us listen and hear.

Mathematics teacher Sally Keyes assigns her seventh graders at Jane Lathrop Stanford Middle School in Palo Alto, California, a "menu" of complex story problems. Once students have completed the menu, she asks them to revisit the process of solving the problems. She gives them the following reflections form she has created, and suggests that they use it to record their thoughts.

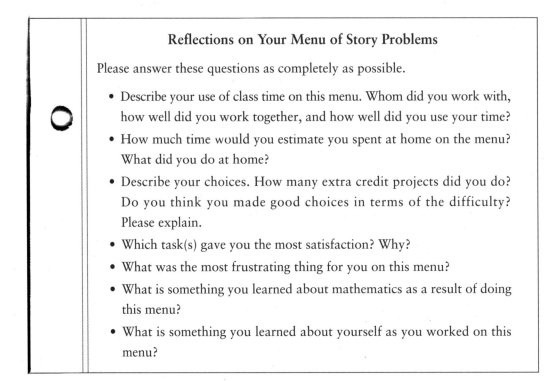

Reflections on Your Menu of Story Problems

Please answer these questions as completely as possible.

- Describe your use of class time on this menu. Whom did you work with, how well did you work together, and how well did you use your time?
- How much time would you estimate you spent at home on the menu? What did you do at home?
- Describe your choices. How many extra credit projects did you do? Do you think you made good choices in terms of the difficulty? Please explain.
- Which task(s) gave you the most satisfaction? Why?
- What was the most frustrating thing for you on this menu?
- What is something you learned about mathematics as a result of doing this menu?
- What is something you learned about yourself as you worked on this menu?

In a similar manner, Toby Kahn Curry, a middle-grade teacher at the Dewey Learning Center in Detroit, Michigan, asks her students to complete the form, "Thinking About Myself as a Learner," at the end of each semester. Once they've completed the form, Curry asks them to create a Learning Plan in which they outline for themselves how they might revise their work strategies to make more productive use of their classroom learning time.

Thinking About Myself as a Learner

Name _____ Date _____ Grade_____

Please write thoughtful, honest answers for this evaluation. Remember, you are the best source for evaluating your own learning. Only you know what you knew before the school year started, and only you know how much you've learned in the last 20 weeks. I have made many observations about each of you as learners, but your responses on this form are very helpful. Please use lined paper to answer any questions that require additional space.

- Describe the most important thing you learned or accomplished in your research.
- Describe what and how much you have read so far this year.
- Explain what kind of math you have worked on.
- Describe the different kinds of writing you have done so far this school year.
- How do you like working in collaborative groups with your classmates?
- What assignments or experiences did you most enjoy this school year?
- What did you least enjoy about the first semester?
- If you could change something about the way our room is organized, what would it be?
- How do you hope to improve upon your learning during the second semester?

Learning logs. Donald Graves (1991) leaves no doubts as to the self-reflective value of learning logs when he writes, "Learning logs are related to everything you do when you make sense of the world." As students work out the meaning of their discoveries through writing and sketching, learning logs can help them

- become conscious of what is happening to them, both personally and academically
- develop a sense of history as learners, and a place to plan out their futures. What will they do next on their learning odysseys?

While the benefits for students seem indisputable, the benefits for teachers are without question. What teacher wouldn't like to see inside her students' heads? You come close to doing just that when you invite your students to keep logs and make sense of their experiences. As you read through your students' logs, you get an inside look at your students' developing logic. You can see why they chose to solve a problem the way they did, or what they thought of a book they read, or how Isadora Duncan influenced a dance they choreographed. You see what they know. You see what they need. And you can plan instruction and create curriculum that will extend and refine their understanding.

As you invite your students to write and sketch their way into understanding across the curriculum, you'll discover that learning logs have multiple benefits.

Learning logs as a tool for problem solving. In their logs, students can jot down things they don't understand. They can also write what they think the problem is, and how they might go about solving it. In the process, they may write their way into understanding.

Ten-year-old Erica was asked to make a dollar out of thirteen coins. In her learning log, she explains how she went about solving the problem.

With learning logs, students write and sketch their way into understanding across the curriculum.

Math puzzle

Make a dollar out of thirteen coins.

MY ANSWER

It was challenging, but it was worth it, and I had a lot of fun!!! Well, I got a peice of paper and a pencil, I made four circles at the left edge in a line going down Then I wrote the numbers 25 in one circle 10 in one circle, five in one circle, and one in the last circle. Then I made about four circles after each one. (Example) Then I put a dot in a circle in the 25th section. then I put a dot in the ten section. And I kept on picking numbers and making dots and then I counted it up and... bingo! I had my answer.

I shared it with...
I shared this math puzzle with my mom.

Learning logs as a tool for reflecting and evaluating. "Writing," the Russian psychologist Lev Vygotsky (1986) once said, "forces shadows of the mind into articulate thought." I used to end every class by asking my students to take out their learning logs and to spend some quiet time reflecting on what they learned that day. Writing requires students to summarize information or ideas they learned, and to consider questions that still remained.

Lauren Montgomery, a nine year old in Rena Malkofsky's elementary classroom in Palo Alto, California, used her science log to summarize what she had learned about building a double electrical circuit.

SWITCHES

ML: Battery lightbulb, light bulb holder, paper clip, rubber band, 2 brads, 3 wires and a piece of tag board with 2 holes in it (▣)

PR: We tried out lots of different ways, then we walked around and looked at the ways that other people were making the switch, and finally did this.

There are many ways to report out and share learning with parents, students, and others. Here's a brief thumbnail sketch of how some educators are using multimedia to share evaluation data.

Audiotapes. Primary teacher Pam Anderson at Orin School in Redwood City, California, tapes her students reading aloud from a book of their choice four times a year. She also tapes her discussion with the children about their responses to the book and their retelling of the story. The tapes are stored at school to guard against loss. After their teacher-parent conference, parents are invited to listen to the tapes in another classroom while Pam starts to conference with another parent. Parents get a very clear picture of their child's developing reading ability as they listen to the tape. They are able to evaluate what they are hearing because Pam conducts parent workshops on the reading process. The parents in Pam's classroom understand that *miscues* (an unexpected response to the text) are a normal part of the reading process (Goodman, Watson and Burke 1987). Miscues that do not interfere with meaning are of no concern, but simply reveal that the child is working effectively to construct meaning from the text. Miscues that do interfere with meaning should be corrected by the child.

Videotapes. Inspired by the innovative practices of Project Zero at Harvard University, Harrington Elementary School teachers in Cambridge, Massachusetts, ask their students' parents to send a blank videotape to school. These tapes are used throughout the school year to capture on video each student's work. Much of the work at Harrington centers on student inquiry and project work. Students may spend days or even weeks interviewing family members and creating oral histories, designing science experiments to test pollution in the drainage ditch behind their school, or creating a school mural representing the cultural diversity of their school community. Through these projects, students show that they know how to pose questions, develop ideas, experiment with possible solutions, and revise, refine, and present their work. The complexity of thinking and understanding in which students engage cannot be stuffed into pencil and paper, fill-in-the-blank tests. Accordingly, as students give oral, dramatic, musical, or scientific presentations, teachers videotape the performances. Students take the tape home and share it with their families. They are also asked to write a self-evaluation of their work and final presentation. What did they think went well? What didn't work as well? What might they do next? Parents also comment and the written evaluations are stored in accordion files together with the videotapes.

What's key here is that the focus is not just on completing the project and getting a grade. Once the project is completed, students revisit it and think how it might be used to explore new questions (Zessoules and Gardner 1991).

DIALOGUE

Reflection brings the learning cycle full circle; and yet ironically, time to think, process, and absorb learning is often left out in the rush to cover the curriculum. Much better to "uncover" the curriculum, as educator Hilda Taba recommended decades ago, and give students the gift of quiet self-reflection and evaluation.

How do I build time into my classroom for student reflection?

_____

_____

How do I support students in their efforts to confer and reflect together?

_____

_____

How do I support student self-reflection?

☐ self-reflective forms?
☐ portfolios?
☐ reflective classroom discussions?
☐ end-of-the-day reflective journal time?

How do I find time every day for my own self-reflection?

_____

_____

In a similar way, the videotapes are not just shown once and stored, but are shown again and again as a basis for discussion regarding standards of excellence and performance. Students are encouraged to

- create projects regularly and frequently. They don't just paint one self-portrait, choreograph one dance, or write one poem. They create again and again, exploring multiple aspects of each discipline.
- engage in continual self-reflection and evaluation throughout the creative process, rather than simply judge the final project. Much of the self-reflection centers on learning logs that students keep to direct, monitor, and document their progress.

- collaborate with others throughout the process of creating a performance or project, and engage in lively discussions about what elements to include, and how best to shape the elements to tell a story or share information.

- understand how the needs of a real audience necessarily shape their presentations. What does the audience need to know? How will they learn it?

- think about their development across time. These students know their history as learners and have a sense of their future as learners. They have goals and understand how they might achieve them.

- understand standards of excellence and strive to improve their own work. Getting a product done is not the goal; creating something of beauty, perhaps even brilliance, and pushing it beyond the limits of their last effort is what compels these students to try and try again.

DIALOGUE

Conduct a quick survey of the assessment tools you are using and the data they yield.

_____

_____

What are the advantages of the assessment tools I use?

_____

_____

Photographs. Primary teacher Denise Ogren who teaches at Stinesville Elementary School in Stinesville, Indiana, has added a new dimension to her students' portfolios—photo reflections. She takes photographs of her students at work, and then later, asks them to reflect on the photograph by answering three questions.

- What are you doing in this photograph?
  - Why do we do that at school?
  - What did you learn from doing this?

In one photograph, two five year olds, Brandon and Stephen, were working with the math junk boxes making patterns. In response to Ogren's questions, the boys explained what they were doing.

Brandon said "I'm playing with the keys. I was putting them out in a special way—circle, straight, circle, straight—a pattern. We do that because we learn stuff and how to make stuff." While Stephen responded "I'm working at math games. I'm doing tools. I was putting this one over there with the other two to make a pattern."

Ogren finds that the photo reflections provide her with yet another way to access her students' thinking. She is able to discover inconsistencies in their logic and plan new curricular experiences that will nudge them into clarifying their understanding. From her experience with Brandon and Stephen, she decided that she needed to help the students connect pattern-making to numbers.

Brandon and Stephen making patterns

Ogren explains:

> My opportunity came when we were learning to count by 5s. I listed multiples of 5 on the board vertically, starting with number 5 and ending with 30. I covered the one's column and asked the children what they saw: 11223—a pattern. We then figured out the next number without counting our fingers, but by using the pattern.

Field Notes: Teacher-To-Teacher

Rather than develop a quiz of what I would like my students to know, I simply ask, "What have you learned?" Their responses vary widely, as I invite them to tell me what they feel is significant about their learning experiences. Students do better in this alternative to quizzes or tests because they all have something to share. Each Friday we take out our learning journals and write down what we learned that week. As we are getting started, I ask who would like to share something they have learned. We continue to discuss the topic until we have explored the specific details involved. Through these weekly discussions, the students learn to give examples and details of their learning. Instead of general comments such as, "I learned about math," they explain, "I learned a new math game with fraction bars that helped me understand how fractions work."

Debra Goodman
Dewey Learning Center
Detroit, Michigan

The complexity of the human mind and learning demands assessment tools that are equally fluid and flexible. If you embrace authentic assessment, you will want to use many different assessment tools: interviews, questionnaires, learning logs, portfolios, videotapes, and the like. You'll also want to invite students and parents to work with you. And you'll want to use the tools from a variety of perspectives as you observe your students at work, interact with them, and analyze the products of their learning. Authentic assessment, just like learning, is multi-dimensional and evolving. We want to document, as richly as possible, the full extent of our students' learning and development, including the dimensions of their understanding which too often remain hidden unless we ask them to engage in open self-reflection.

D I A L O G U E

What revisions could be made to the assessment tools I use to encourage my students to be self-evaluators? What additional assessment tools might I use?

_____

_____

_____

How do I use authentic assessment to evaluate what and how I teach?

_____

_____

_____

How do my colleagues assess their students? their teaching strategies?

_____

_____

_____

Beyond evaluating what simply exists now, we are also interested in what might evolve next. In other words, we want to explore the transformations in students' development; how they are outgrowing their current selves. "Powerful assessment," suggest Zessoules and Gardner (1991) "must also capture how… new understandings metamorphose."

SHOPTALK

Bridges Bird, Lois, Kenneth S. Goodman and Yetta M. Goodman, eds. *The Whole Language Catalog: Forms for Authentic Assessment.* New York: SRA: Macmillan/McGraw-Hill, 1994.

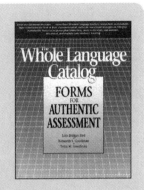

Professor Dorothy Watson says that "Whole language teachers share their best," and indeed, within this book you'll find the best of authentic assessment forms and strategies developed by more than 50 educators. These are forms they've created and use in their classrooms to monitor, document, report on, and evaluate a range of authentic learning experiences in which their students are engaged. The book is easy to use. Each form (ready for photocopying) is accompanied by a description explaining who the form is most appropriate for, why it was created, and how to use it. Additional information under "What Else?" may add to the utility of the forms.

Eggleton, Jill. *Whole Language Evaluation: Reading, Writing and Spelling.* Botheld, Washington: The Wright Group, 1990.

The aim of this book, as stated in the foreword, is to bridge the gap between what is currently known about language learning and teaching and evaluation. It provides useful guidelines for observing and recording children's developing literacy strategies. What the book lacks in theoretical explanations, it makes up for in theoretically sound forms and checklists that are easy to replicate for classroom use. This book works well for those starting to use authentic assessment, and for those who already know a lot about it and can use the forms as points of departure for creating their own.

S H O P T A L K

Perrone, Vito, ed. *Expanding Student Assessment*. Alexandria, Virginia: Association for Supervision and Curriculum Development, 1991.

Expanding Student Assessment

Edited by
Vito Perrone

As the former director of the University of North Dakota Study Group, Vito Perrone has long been at the forefront of the movement to develop more authentic means of assessing children's language and learning. Perrone points out that the roots of authentic assessment extend back decades to the progressive schools influenced by the work of John Dewey, John Kilpatrick, and Caroline Pratt, among others. In this collection of ten essays, you'll be treated to a mix of classroom practices (portfolios, documentation, exhibitions) and theoretical exploration. A common thread runs through each essay: Authentic assessment is the lifeblood of responsive teaching. For those who want to analyze and change the nature of educational evaluation, the message is clear—enter classrooms and observe teachers and students at work. Once there, this important volume will guide, inspire, and challenge.

Chapter 4

Purposeful Portfolios

Student self-evaluation may well lie at the heart of effective education. By stepping back from their work and considering it carefully, students gain new insights and ideas about themselves as learners. They come to understand their work in relation to others, and learn how to build on their strengths. With time and practice, students learn to recognize the new possibilities and challenges inherent in their work that may lead them in new learning directions.

But real student self-evaluation is not something that is just tucked in at the end of a thematic unit or brought out at report card time. In order to be effective, students should be involved in continuous self-reflection and evaluation across the curriculum. Indeed, Zessoules and Gardner (1991) urge students to develop "reflective habits of mind."

What can you do to help students engage in self-reflection as a natural habit?

- Provide frequent opportunities for self-reflection.
- Offer students multiple tools to use for self-evaluation such as self-evaluation forms, learning logs, portfolios, self-reflective letters, and daily reflective classroom discussions.
- Demonstrate your own self-reflection and evaluation. Show your students how you use the insights you gain from introspection to shape, refine, and extend your further learning.

Portfolios offer unique opportunities for self-reflection and sensitive, in-depth learning and teaching. Traditional measures like report cards and end-of-the-semester tests tend to spotlight students' weaknesses. Portfolios shift that focus. They are powerful learning tools, helping students discover their strengths, their potentials, and possible directions for new learning.

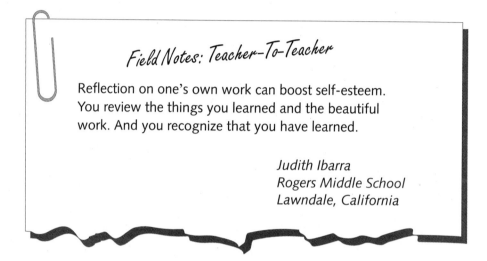

Field Notes: Teacher-To-Teacher

Reflection on one's own work can boost self-esteem. You review the things you learned and the beautiful work. And you recognize that you have learned.

Judith Ibarra
Rogers Middle School
Lawndale, California

The benefits of portfolios for all are numerous.

- For you, portfolios reveal the depth and breadth of your students' developing knowledge and understanding. Within your students' portfolios, you'll find their evolving learning stories—what their interests are, their strengths, their needs, and the nature of instructional support they need to enter new realms of knowing.

- For students, portfolios encourage the sort of active, purposeful thinking that characterizes effective learning—identifying questions, setting goals, exploring a variety of resources, self-monitoring progress, sharing the results of learning, reflecting back on what's been learned, how it's been learned, what worked, what didn't, and beginning again with new questions and goals.

- For administrators, portfolios provide concrete evidence and documentation of student learning, of the subject area content that's been explored, and of the extent to which instructional goals have been achieved.

- For parents, portfolios offer reassurance that their children are learning. Unlike rows of grades on a report card, portfolios showcase the full spectrum of student development and ability. Parents can see exactly what and how their children are learning. Perhaps most importantly, as parents read their children's self-evaluative comments, they'll learn how their children view themselves as learners.

Just like the term authentic assessment, *portfolio* means different things to different people. It may bring to mind everything from a dog-eared manila folder stuffed with gold-starred worksheets to a leather-grained, professional artist's portfolio containing a range and depth of striking watercolors. Our understanding of what portfolios are and how they should be used in classrooms is necessarily evolving. "We need to explore the many uses of portfolios for at least another five years, and perhaps indefinitely," cautions Donald Graves and Bonnie Sunstein (1992). "Without careful exploration, portfolio use is doomed to failure. They will be too quickly tried, found wanting, and just as quickly abandoned."

A real portfolio, however, involves the student. What separates a potpourri of student work from a purposeful representation of student development and understanding is student participation and self-evaluation. Thus, the definition Paulson, Paulson and Meyer (1991) offer in their article "What Makes a Portfolio a Portfolio?" is one we might live with while we continue to explore all the possibilities of portfolio use.

Our understanding of what portfolios are and how they should be used in classrooms is necessarily evolving.

> A portfolio is a purposeful collection of student work that exhibits the student's efforts, progress, and achievements in one or more areas. The collection must include student participation in selecting contents, the criteria for selection, the criteria for judging merit, and evidence of student self-reflection.

Field Notes: Teacher-To-Teacher

We talked about literacy as the process of knowing ourselves and our world... the purpose of portfolios also can be to get to know ourselves better.

Wendy Motoike Inman
Encinita Elementary School
Rosemead, California

I recommend that you take time to experiment with portfolios in your own way and discover how they work best for you and your students. The most effective use of portfolios begins with thoughtful consideration of a range of issues surrounding their design and purpose, beginning, perhaps, with the questions: Why do I want to use portfolios? What do I hope to accomplish?

Used in a thoughtful manner, portfolios can serve as the focal point for teaching, learning, and reflection for both teachers and students. But *doing* portfolios and *learning with* portfolios are two very different things. I've developed "Learning With Portfolios—Guidelines" to help you get started. Spend some time with your colleagues thinking through the points I've listed. Successful portfolio implementation begins with reflection. I offer my recommendations, but, ultimately, you'll want to do what makes sense for you and your students. You will also want to consider your district requirements for portfolio use.

Learning With Portfolios—Guidelines

What should go in the portfolio? Portfolios are powerful learning tools. I recommend that students include their works in progress, evolving drafts as well as final, polished pieces. The nuances of student development are not obvious in final products only.

Who will contribute to the portfolio? I believe that students should select and control the contents of their portfolios. I also think that they should justify in some reflective way (either verbally or nonverbally), why they want to include each entry. You may want to recommend some selections that you think showcase a particular strategy or ability. As portfolios are a personal statement about each student's learning journey, I believe that learners should have complete ownership of their portfolios.

Successful portfolio implementation begins with reflection.

What will my students use to hold the contents of their portfolios? Portfolios can take many forms. You'll need to decide which format will work best for you and your students. You may want to require a uniform container or let each student design his or her own. Listed below are some possibilities.

- accordion file
- three-hole binder
- manila folder
- large boot box
- commercial portfolio (a variety are now available through educational publishers)

What will students include in their portfolios? This may be completely open-ended, limited only by the physical dimensions of the portfolio and storage constraints. Here is a list of possible inclusions:

- questions, issues, brainstorming, notes associated with research projects
- sketches, diagrams, semantic maps
- photographs the student has taken; photographs of the student at work
- rough drafts, works of written and visual arts compositions in progress
- published books, polished drawings, paintings
- videotapes of student presentations

- peer, teacher, and parent feedback
- lists of books the student has read
- comments from student about the books
- list of people with whom the student shared the books
- audiotapes of the student reading; student may record reading once a month and include a self-evaluation of the reading
- reflection on peer, teacher, and parent feedback
- miscue analysis
- literature logs
- lists of literature studies in which the student has participated
- lists of research projects in which the student has participated
- descriptions of reading, writing, math, science, research strategies the student controls
- lists of skills and conventions the student controls across math, science, language arts, visual and performing arts
- personal reflections on experiences
- self-evaluations

How will students review and revise their portfolios? I recommend that you schedule a regular time for portfolio selection and review by the children at least every two weeks. You may want to do this as a whole-class activity or meet with small groups of students.

Norman Brown, who teaches visual arts and has been experimenting with Arts Propel "process-folios," reports that the review process is the most valuable constant in his classroom. Brown (1989) explains:

While [portfolio review] may originally have occurred once or twice throughout a semester, it now occurs on a continual, ongoing basis. It has become very much

a part of every student evaluation, as well as something students are taught to do for themselves. Portfolio review may begin with a student laying out every piece of work done over a week, a month, or a semester. We may do this as a class, using a critique format, or individually, face-to-face, teacher and student.

How will I engage students in self-evaluation? Portfolios are purposeful, self-reflective tools for learning. They are not a potpourri, hodge-podge collection of student work. What separates a portfolio from a simple collection is self-evaluation. It's worth noting again that self-evaluation, in fact, is the key component of portfolio assessment. I suggest two options depending on the age and developmental abilities of your students.

1. Students write a self-evaluative paragraph for each entry explaining why they chose to include the entry and what it shows about their developing ability. Young children can dictate their explanations, or draw pictures to tell a story about their understandings and insights.

2. Students complete a simple form and clip it to each entry.

   • Why I chose this entry.

   • What it shows about me as a learner.

   • My learning goals.

This form can be adapted to include pictures that young children circle or, in some way, graphically indicate their self-evaluation.

Karolynne Gee, a visual arts specialist and Director of Professional Development at the Galef Institute, asks her students to choose work that shows who they are as artists (forthcoming). As students consider what to put in their artist's portfolios, they complete these open-ended sentences:

   • This art piece makes me feel _____

   • I chose this art piece because it shows that I _____

SHOPTALK

Tierney, Robert, Mark Carter and Laura Desai. *Portfolio Assessment in the Reading-Writing Classroom*. Norwood, Massachusetts: Christopher-Gordon, 1991.

In reviewing this book, Richard J. Meyer, professor of education at the University of Nebraska, writes "A teacher choosing to use portfolios for assessment is making a statement about the kind of classroom he or she is participating in with children. Portfolios are linked to a spirit or way of being with children. Portfolios are not simply a dumping ground for everything that a child has read, responded to, or written. Most of the teachers showcased in this book asked children to keep two folders. One was a collection of all of their written work; the other showed their progress over time. Teachers and students engaged in collaborative evaluation, discussing the growth and changes each had seen over a period of time, as they decided together which compositions and projects should be placed in the students' portfolios. The book's many flowcharts, diagrams, and reproducible checklists will aid teachers as they incorporate portfolios into their classrooms and tackle the important issue of accountability. Portfolios are essential for teachers who want to design classrooms that support learning and growth, and who want to know as much as they can about their students—in the most efficient way possible."

How will I evaluate the portfolio? What criteria will I use? Here is a list you might consider:

- evidence of the student's risk-taking
- flexibility as a learner; ability to use multiple modalities for a variety of purposes
- revising, editing, and experimenting with different learning modes
- ability to refine and elaborate upon meaning; shows developing control over conventions
- awareness of student's own thinking
- ability to pose questions
- ability to find answers to questions, use of a variety of resources
- self-reflection on teacher and peer feedback
- self-assessment; ability to establish and use criteria to evaluate the process and products of learning.

How will I use the portfolios to establish educational goals for each child?
Portfolios may be most effective when you can meet with each student and
discuss the contents of the portfolio. What is the student learning? What is
working well? What isn't working as well? What direction should the student take next? I recommend that you meet with each student at least once
per grading period, and, if possible, involve both the child and his or her parents in a goal-setting conference. Some teachers like to make a simple form
for students to use during the conference.

- My learning goals _____
- My parents' goals _____
- My teacher's goals _____

How should I share the portfolios with parents? Elizabeth Hebert, the principal of Crow Island School in Winnetka, Illinois, has led her faculty in the
development of "Portfolio Evenings," a time when parents and family members are invited to the school for a review and celebration of their child's
portfolio. Hebert explains how the evening works (1994).

> On Portfolio Evenings, which last for about an hour and a half, the chil-
> dren sit with their parents and present their portfolios. The teachers and
> principal circulate, visiting each student and highlighting particular mile-
> stones that each youngster may have attained. Teachers and principal are
> available for questions but try not to intrude because it's really the chil-
> dren's evening, and they need to run the show as much as possible. Parents
> and teachers have been impressed with the leadership and independence
> that even the youngest students have demonstrated in this setting.

In preparation for the Portfolio Evening, the children are asked to review
their portfolios and work with their teachers to complete the reflective
questionnaire shown on the next page. In addition to the portfolio sharing,
Crow Island students and teachers also complete the "Learning Experiences
Form." Influenced by Howard Gardner's *Frames of Mind* (1983), the Crow
Island faculty designed the form so that
it reflects the multiple dimensions of a
child's learning. The form also provides
space for the student's self-reflection.
Older students write their own
thoughts; teachers take dictation
from younger students.
Parents are encouraged
to add their reflective
comments as well.

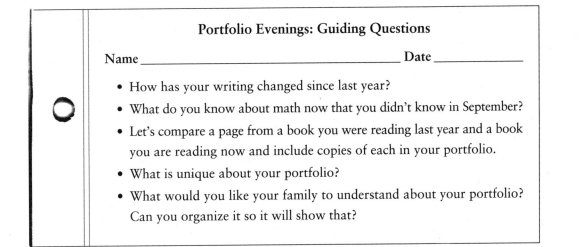

Portfolio Evenings: Guiding Questions

Name _____ Date _____

- How has your writing changed since last year?
- What do you know about math now that you didn't know in September?
- Let's compare a page from a book you were reading last year and a book you are reading now and include copies of each in your portfolio.
- What is unique about your portfolio?
- What would you like your family to understand about your portfolio? Can you organize it so it will show that?

Learning Experiences Form

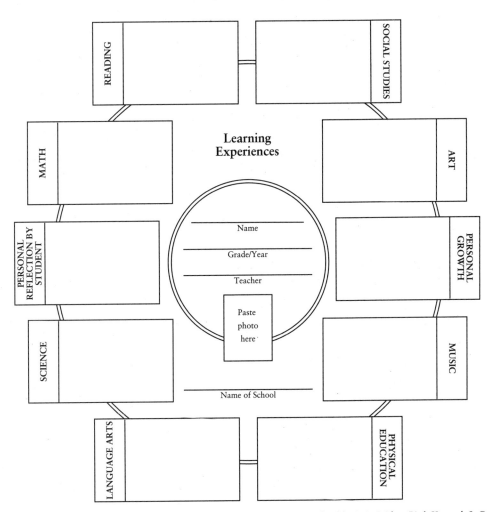

The Whole Language Catalog: Forms for Authentic Assessment © 1994 edited by Lois Bridges Bird, Kenneth S. Goodman and Yetta M. Goodman

If time and space constraints would make a Portfolio Evening impossible in your school, you might consider simply sending the portfolio home with the student. To ensure that parents spend time looking at the portfolio with their child, you might request that they write and return their reflection and review of the portfolio contents with the portfolio.

When my oldest daughter was in sixth grade, she kept an extensive math and science portfolio that she brought home to share with our family twice a year. She opened her portfolio with a "Dear Reader" letter explaining what we would see as we looked through her portfolio as well as how she felt about each entry and what her learning goals were for herself as a mathematician and scientist. In her letter, she asked us to write a letter back to her, sharing our insights and ideas about her growing mathematical and scientific understanding. At the back of her portfolio, we read this letter from her teacher.

Dear Parents and Readers,

Thank you for reading your child's portfolio. The portfolio is the product of a great deal of time and effort on the part of the student and is a way to reflect on his or her accomplishments in sixth grade math and science. From reading their entries in the portfolio, it is clear how students gain a better awareness of the scope of their learning over the year and how they benefit from the opportunity to review some parts of the math and science curriculum. The entries show that students not only develop an awareness of what they have learned, but also of themselves as learners: with individual strengths and needs, prior learning histories, and personal learning styles.

Since the beginning of the year, the students have explored many topics in math and science and have gained considerable content knowledge in these areas. The sections on math computation and concepts and science content reflect this progress. Equally important, they have become much more proficient at the processes of learning and reporting in math and science. The sections on math problem solving and communication and the scientific method show their understandings of problem solving and investigations in math and science.

I hope you are able to read this portfolio and the work folders with your child and share with them their accomplishments over the past year. Please record your comments on the other side of this page and be sure to sign the bottom. Thank you.

Sincerely yours,

Christina Althoff
Jane Lathrop Stanford Middle School
Palo Alto, California

Some teachers prefer to give parents an evaluation form to use as they review their child's portfolio. Here's one developed by a teacher I met at a conference which asks parents to respond in some detail to specific questions.

Parent Response to Portfolio

The portfolio is a place where students store and evaluate their work. It is a place to show you who they are as readers, writers, and learners.

Please read through your son's or daughter's portfolio contents.

- What do you notice that he or she is able to do well?
- What impressed you about your son or daughter's portfolio?
- What is your favorite piece? your favorite sentence?
- Did you have any surprises?
- Did the portfolio help you understand your child's progress?
- Do you have any questions?
- What would you like to know more about concerning your child's progress?
- Do you have any goals or suggestions for your child?

Please sign this paper and return it with the portfolio.

Thank you,

M. Coats

Parent's signature_____ Date_____

Student _____

How Should I Implement Portfolios?

Once you've made some decisions about the role of portfolios in your classroom, you might want to think next about how to begin using them. There are many ways to use portfolios. Following the lead of Tierney, Carter, and Desai (1991), I suggest these implementation steps. You'll want to alter them to fit your and your students' unique needs and interests.

Establishing criteria. First you'll want to establish criteria for assessment and portfolio development. Ideally, you'll create and negotiate the criteria with your students. Even young children can begin to think about what's important in their work, and work to achieve it. You may also invite parents to state their educational goals for their children and incorporate them as well.

Building the portfolios. Now students are ready to begin to build and organize their portfolios, using the agreed-upon criteria for selection and self-evaluation. Students may include a self-evaluation form with each selected piece indicating why they chose the piece and what it reveals about them as learners or they may write a brief statement noting the same points.

Reviewing and evaluating. Once you've completed a *Different Ways of Knowing* module, or at the end of a grading period, students review their portfolios and write an evaluative summary detailing what they view as their strengths and future goals ("What I Do Well, What I'm Working On, What I Plan to Learn"). Students then submit their summaries and portfolios to you.

DIALOGUE

If possible, with a group of your colleagues, brainstorm some answers to these questions.

How will I meet and conference with all thirty-some students about their portfolios?

_____

_____

How often should students visit their portfolios? Whenever the need arises, as determined by each student? at regularly scheduled times?

_____

_____

How will I create time for multiple revisits of student portfolios?

_____

_____

Conferencing. If possible, you'll want to conduct an evaluative conference with each student (parents may be included, too) or with small groups of students. Together you'll review the portfolio and the student's self-evaluative comments and summary. Then you'll want to share your assessment of the portfolio. Together, you decide on the next course of action—what goals the student should focus on next and how he or she should go about achieving those goals.

Often in the example of one, lies lessons for many. Sally Keyes from Jane Lathrop Stanford Middle School in Palo Alto, California, uses "Your Math Portfolio" form to help her math students evaluate what they are learning.

Your Math Portfolio

I. Introduction

This is an introduction to your portfolio. Write this as a friendly letter addressed to "Dear portfolio reader." In this letter you should include (in separate paragraphs):

- a description of what this portfolio is
- a description of what your mathematics class is like
- a description of what you are like in math class.

(Be sure to sign your letter! 10 points)

II. Work Selections

Please include selections of work in the following categories. Staple a gray half-sheet of paper to each piece and describe your thinking (in ink). Be sure to be thoughtful, thorough, and neat.

- Something that was interesting to you
- Something that shows competence with a mathematical tool
- Something you did with a partner or group
- Something you enjoyed
- Something that shows your mathematical thinking (how you solve problems)
- Something you want to improve on or learn more about

(5 points)

III. Reflections Worksheet

Complete these sentences thoughtfully, thoroughly, and neatly. (See the "Math Reflections" essay on page 101 that one student wrote in response to these 10 sentences.)

- I'm proud that...
- I need to work...
- Working in small groups is...
- My favorite assignment so far was...
- I'm getting better at...
- I feel really good about myself when...
- The most difficult problem I solved was...
- Something I still don't understand is...
- I'm still not sure how to do...
- One thing I want to learn more about is...

(10 points)

IV. Goals

How can you improve your mathematical power? What are specific things you can do to become more mathematically powerful and confident? How will you try to achieve these goals?

(10 points)

V. Presentation

Your portfolio needs to be in a report folder. It should include the following in order:

- A cover sheet titled "First Mathematics Portfolio of Seventh Grade," your name, date, and period, and graphics (optional)
- Your introduction
- Your work selections in order
- Your goals

(5 points including neatness)

This portfolio is due on _____. It is worth 65 points! For each part of the portfolio, you will get part or all of the points depending upon the thoroughness of your work.

We will be presenting these portfolios to our parents. Getting a written response from your parents is extra credit! We will be talking more about this later.

Have fun, and make a portfolio you can be proud to share!

Determining instructional goals. You'll want to write a narrative summary for each student conference describing or listing your curriculum and instructional goals for the student. These goals will determine the sorts of instructional support you need to provide. You'll find that you will be asking yourself, "How can I use the information I've gained from my students' portfolios to encourage further learning?"

Guidelines for mathematics portfolios. How do students respond? My daughter, Aislinn, is a student in Sally Keyes's classroom. She has grown from a student who completed her math assignments with little understanding, to one who now not only enjoys math, but also understands it. And best of all, she knows that when she doesn't understand a new concept, she can turn to a variety of strategies (including talking with the teacher) to achieve understanding.

Aislinn wrote a reflective essay after putting her portfolio together. As her essay on the next page shows, students who are routinely invited to evaluate their own learning processes can articulate their strengths and needs.

In addition to the reflective essay in which students evaluate their overall mathematical progress, they must also write a reflective note about each entry they select to put in their portfolio. Below is a sample from Aislinn's portfolio in which she explains why she chose a Problem of the Week that required her to write an involved essay describing her problem-solving process.

> This assignment was a P.O.W. On a P.O.W. we get a problem. Then once we have the answer we write about it. On this one there was a girl coming home from trick-or-treating. On her way home a ghost took ½ of her candy plus 2 more, they attacked 3 times. We had to find out how much candy she had left.
> I think this piece shows how I think the best, and I wanted to have a P.O.W in here, too. I had to make a chart to figure it out. And it took a lot of thinking to get the answer.

As you consider trying portfolios in your room, allow yourself and your students time to experiment. Just as the contents of the portfolios change, revealing the evolution of student thinking and development, so too will the process you follow as you and your students engage in this exciting form of assessment.

Aislinn's Math Reflections

I'm proud that I'm doing so well in math. My grade is very good at an A. I'm very proud about that. The work I'm doing in math is very good, too. I'm learning a lot and having fun which makes it a lot easier. Overall I think this math class is going very well. I feel very good about math this year.

I need to work more on my multiplication. I know most of it, but not right off the top of my head, which makes it hard to do division. So I really, really need to work on it. Because you use multiplication every day. And you can't do a lot more if you don't know it. The hardest part for me is just getting it into my head.

Working in small groups is very good for me. I can work better with more people and learn more. It is easier and more helpful if all the people work hard. And with most of the groups I have been in, everyone works very hard. So if you are with the right people it is very helpful, but if you aren't, it does not help at all.

My favorite assignment so far was doing the Isometric Dot Paper activities. I found it a lot of fun connecting the dots, and following the directions to get the shape. It was like a secret code that you were trying to break. I just found it a lot of fun.

I am getting much better at adding and subtracting fractions. Last year, and at the beginning of the year, I had a very hard time with it. I just did not get how to do it; it did not make sense to me. But after I practiced it and did them on "Problems To Do," I got the hang of it and started understanding it. Now I know how to do it and understand it.

I feel really good about myself when I get a really hard problem right. Some of the POWs [Problem of the Week] I've had have been very hard. And I work very hard to get the answer. If I get the answer right, I feel very good about myself because I proved to myself that I do hard things and do it right.

The most difficult problem I solved was the Budgie POW because I had to use algebra which I did not understand. The hardest part for me was getting started and after that, it did not get much easier. Part of the problem was that my dad took over the problem. And then he did not know how to tell me what he did in a way that I could understand. But I finally did it myself and got an A-!

Something I still don't understand is the Estimating Fractional Parts sheet. I just did not get it. Several people tried to help me, and I got the answers. But I don't understand how and why I got what I got. So I need to work on that.

I'm still not sure how to do the graphing. I know what to do once I have the numbers and where to put them. But I always forget if the Y goes first or the X goes first. It is just something I keep forgetting.

One thing I want to learn more about is algebra, because it looks very interesting. I have done a little bit of it, but not much. It probably is easier than it looks, but right now it looks pretty hard. Still, I really want to learn it.

Aislinn Bird

With time, perhaps you'll agree with seventh-grade teacher Jean Diamond, who has been exploring portfolios in her language arts and social studies classes at Muscatel Middle School in Rosemead, California. Diamond writes:

> My students and I find portfolios invaluable. The students' portfolio folders are passed out several times a week and collected in order, so a great many hours of shuffling and recording is eliminated. Students have developed skills of self-evaluation and peer evaluation through their sharing of portfolios. It becomes a matter of great pride when students are empowered through reflection to become their own standard-setters and judges. Portfolios make wonderful tools for parent conferences. They are a graphic means of seeing what the class does, and what individual students do. It's hard to argue with an empty folder next to choice work. As far as I'm concerned there are no misuses to portfolios. They save time and help students, teachers, and parents assess progress by review and reflection.

In closing, portfolios can be bright windows on the mind, revealing thinking and learning in ways few assessment tools can. Portfolios enable us "to know the direction we are going [and] the strategies we need to get there," encouraging us to become the "authors of our own lives" (Short and Burke 1991).

SHOPTALK

Drummond, Mary Jane. *Learning To See: Assessment Through Observation.* York, Maine: Stenhouse Publishers, 1994.

Why do you assess your students' work? Obvious reasons aside (because you're required to and parents expect information about their child's learning), Drummond helps us understand the real value of assessment—to learn, to inform our teaching, to guide our observations of our students so that we can plan more sensitive instruction and stimulating curriculum. Drummond also helps us understand that we can not separate our personal values from our assessments. To that end, she urges us to be ever-respectful and truthful of our students, to "understand learning with intense professional commitment…" Readers of this provocative book will come away with a new understanding of teaching and perhaps, new pride in their ability to meet its amazing challenge.

Professional Bibliography

Anthony, Robert J., Terry D. Johnson, Norma I. Mickelson and Alison Preece. *Evaluating Literacy: A Perspective for Change.* Portsmouth, New Hampshire: Heinemann, 1991.

Armstrong, Thomas. *Multiple Intelligences in the Classroom.* Alexandria, Virginia: Association for Supervision and Curriculum Development, 1994.

Atwell, Nancie. *In the Middle: Writing, Reading, and Learning with Adolescents.* Portsmouth, New Hampshire: Heinemann, 1987.

Barr, Mary. *The California Learning Record: Handbook for Teachers K-6.* Sacramento: California State Department of Education, 1994.

Barr, Myra, Sue Ellis, Hilary Hester and Anne Thomas. *The Primary Language Record.* Portsmouth, New Hampshire: Heinemann, 1988.

Bridges, Lois. *Creating Your Classroom Community.* Strategies for Teaching and Learning Professional Library, The Galef Institute. York, Maine: Stenhouse Publishers, 1995.

Bridges Bird, Lois. *Becoming a Whole Language School: The Fair Oaks Story.* Katonah, New York: Richard C. Owen, 1991.

_____. "Whole Language Teachers Do Teach," *The Whole Language Catalog,* edited by Kenneth S. Goodman, Lois Bridges Bird and Yetta M. Goodman. New York: SRA: Macmillan/McGraw-Hill, 1991.

Bridges Bird, Lois, Kenneth S. Goodman and Yetta M. Goodman, eds. *The Whole Language Catalog: Forms for Authentic Assessment.* New York: SRA: Macmillan/McGraw-Hill, 1994.

Brown, Norman. "Portfolio Reviews: Pivots, Companions and Footprints," *Portfolio, The Newsletter for Arts Propel,* February 1989.

Burke, Carolyn. "The Burke Reading Interview," *Reading Miscue Inventory: Alternative Procedures,* edited by Yetta M. Goodman, Dorothy Watson and Carolyn Burke. Katonah, New York: Richard C. Owen, 1987.

California State Department of Education. *Prelude to Performance Assessment in the Arts.* Sacramento: California State Department of Education, 1993.

Crafton, Linda. *Whole Language...Getting Started, Moving Forward.* Katonah, New York: Richard C. Owen, 1991.

Daly, Elizabeth, ed. *Monitoring Children's Language Development: Holistic Assessment in the Classroom.* Portsmouth, New Hampshire: Heinemann, 1990.

Drummond, Mary Jane. *Learning To See: Assessment Through Observation.* York, Maine: Stenhouse Publishers, 1994; Markham, Ontario: Pembroke Publishers, 1994.

Eggleton, Jill. *Whole Language Evaluation: Reading, Writing and Spelling.* Botheld, Washington: The Wright Group, 1990.

Gardner, Howard. *Frames of Mind: The Theory of Multiple Intelligences.* New York: Basics Books, 1983.

Gee, Karolynne. *Visual Arts as a Way of Knowing.* Strategies for Teaching and Learning Professional Library, The Galef Institute. York, Maine: Stenhouse Publishers (forthcoming).

Goodman, Kenneth S., Lois Bridges Bird and Yetta M. Goodman, eds. *The Whole Language Catalog: Supplement on Authentic Assessment.* New York: SRA: Macmillan/McGraw-Hill, 1992.

Goodman, Kenneth S. "The Case of the Vanishing Checklists," *The Whole Language Catalog: Supplement on Authentic Assessment,* edited by Kenneth S. Goodman, Lois Bridges Bird and Yetta M. Goodman. New York: SRA: Macmillan/McGraw-Hill, 1992.

Goodman, Yetta M. "Reversals —slasreveR," *The Whole Language Catalog,* edited by Kenneth S. Goodman, Lois Bridges Bird and Yetta M. Goodman. New York: SRA: Macmillan/McGraw-Hill, 1991.

_____. "Kidwatching: An Alternative to Testing," *The National Elementary Principal,* November 1978.

Goodman, Yetta, Dorothy Watson and Carolyn Burke. *Reading Miscue Inventory: Alternative Procedures*. Katonah, New York: Richard C. Owen, 1987.

Graves, Donald and Bonnie Sunstein. *Portfolio Portraits*. Portsmouth, New Hampshire: Heinemann, 1992.

Graves, Donald. *The Reading/Writing Teacher's Companion: Investigate Nonfiction*. Portsmouth, New Hampshire: Heinemann, 1991.

Hebert, Elizabeth. "Portfolio Evenings: Guiding Questions," *The Whole Language Catalog: Forms for Authentic Assessment*, edited by Lois Bridges Bird, Kenneth S. Goodman and Yetta M. Goodman. New York: SRA: Macmillan/McGraw-Hill, 1994.

Heller, Paul G. *Drama as a Way of Knowing*. Strategies for Teaching and Learning Professional Library, The Galef Institute. York, Maine: Stenhouse Publishers, 1995.

Johnston, Peter H. *Knowing Literacy: Constructive Literacy Assessment*. York, Maine: Stenhouse Publishers, 1997.

Jones, Peter. "Joshua: An Effective Teacher Developer," *English Language Arts News*. Australian newsletter, no. 4, 1987.

Morgenbesser, Martin. "Teaching as Improvisational Theater," *The Whole Language Catalog*, edited by Kenneth S. Goodman, Lois Bridges Bird and Yetta M. Goodman. New York: SRA: Macmillan/McGraw-Hill, 1991.

Morrissey, Maureen. "When 'Shut Up' Is a Sign of Growth," *The Whole Language Evaluation Book*, edited by Kenneth S. Goodman, Yetta M. Goodman and Wendy Hood. Portsmouth, New Hampshire: Heinemann, 1989.

Ohanian, Susan. *Math as a Way of Knowing*. Strategies for Teaching and Learning Professional Library, The Galef Institute. York, Maine: Stenhouse Publishers, 1995.

Page, Nick. *Music as a Way of Knowing*. Strategies for Teaching and Learning Professional Library, The Galef Institute. York, Maine: Stenhouse Publishers, 1995.

Paulson, Leon, Pearl Paulson and Carol Meyer. "What Makes a Portfolio a Portfolio?" *Educational Leadership*, February 1991.

Perrone, Vito, ed. *Expanding Student Assessment*. Alexandria, Virginia: Association for Supervision and Curriculum Development, 1991.

Roderick, Jessie A., ed. *Context-Responsive Approaches to Assessing Children's Language*. Urbana, Illinois: National Council of Teachers of English, 1991.

Short, Kathy G. and Carolyn Burke. *Creating Curriculum: Teachers and Students as a Community of Learners.* Portsmouth, New Hampshire: Heinemann, 1991.

Silvers, Penny. "Everyday Signs of Learning: Inquiry-Based Evaluation," *Primary Voices K-6,* April 1994.

Taba, Hilda. *Curriculum Development Theory and Practice.* New York: Harcourt, Brace and World, 1962.

Tierney, Robert, Mark Carter and Laura Desai. *Portfolio Assessment in the Reading-Writing Classroom.* Norwood, Massachusetts: Christopher-Gordon, 1991.

Vygotsky, Lev. *Thought and Language.* Cambridge, Massachusetts: MIT Press, 1986.

Watson, Dorothy. "Assessing Children's Language," *Observing the Language Learner,* edited by Angela Jaggar and Trika Burke-Smith. Newark, Delaware: International Reading Association and Urbana, Illinois: National Council of Teachers of English, 1985.

Wolf, Dennie Palmer and Nancy Pistone. *Taking Full Measure: Rethinking Assessment Through the Arts.* New York: College Entrance Examination Board, 1991.

Zessoules, Reineke and Howard Gardner. "Authentic Assessment: Beyond the Buzzword," *Expanding Student Assessment,* edited by Vito Perrone. Alexandria, Virginia: Association for Supervision and Curriculum Development, 1991.

Professional Associations and Publications

The American Alliance for Health, Physical
Education, Recreation, and Dance
(AAHPERD)
*Journal of Physical Education, Recreation,
and Dance*
1900 Association Drive
Reston, Virginia 22091

American Alliance for Theater and Education
(AATE)
AATE Newsletter
c/o Arizona State University Theater Department
Box 873411
Tempe, Arizona 85287

American Association for the Advancement
of Science (AAAS)
Science Magazine
1333 H Street NW
Washington, DC 20005

American Association of Colleges for Teacher
Education (AACTE)
AACTE Briefs
1 DuPont Circle NW, Suite 610
Washington, DC 20036

American Association of School Administrators
(AASA)
The School Administrator
1801 North Moore Street
Arlington, Virginia 22209

Association for Childhood Education
International (ACEI)
*Childhood Education: Infancy Through
Early Adolescence*
11141 Georgia Avenue, Suite 200
Wheaton, Maryland 20902

Association for Supervision and Curriculum
Development (ASCD)
Educational Leadership
1250 North Pitt Street
Alexandria, Virginia 22314

The Council for Exceptional Children (CEC)
Teaching Exceptional Children
1920 Association Drive
Reston, Virginia 22091

Education Theater Association (ETA)
Dramatics
3368 Central Parkway
Cincinnati, Ohio 45225

International Reading Association
(IRA)
The Reading Teacher
800 Barksdale Road
Newark, Delaware 19714

Music Educators National Conference
(MENC)
Music Educators Journal
1806 Robert Fulton Drive
Reston, Virginia 22091

National Art Education Association
(NAEA)
Art Education
1916 Association Drive
Reston, Virginia 22091

National Association for the Education
of Young Children (NAEYC)
Young Children
1509 16th Street NW
Washington, DC 20036

National Association of Elementary
School Principals (NAESP)
Communicator
1615 Duke Street
Alexandria, Virginia 22314

National Center for Restructuring
Education, Schools, and Teaching
(NCREST)
Resources for Restructuring
P.O. Box 110
Teachers College, Columbia University
New York, New York 10027

National Council for the Social Studies
(NCSS)
Social Education
Social Studies and the Young Learner
3501 Newark Street NW
Washington, DC 20016

National Council of Supervisors of
Mathematics (NCSM)
*NCSM Newsletter Leadership in
Mathematics Education*
P.O. Box 10667
Golden, Colorado 80401

National Council of Teachers of
English (NCTE)
Language Arts
Primary Voices K-6
1111 Kenyon Road
Urbana, Illinois 61801

National Council of Teachers of
Mathematics (NCTM)
Arithmetic Teacher
Teaching Children Mathematics
1906 Association Drive
Reston, Virginia 22091

National Dance Association
(NDA)
Spotlight on Dance
1900 Association Drive
Reston, Virginia 22091

National Science Teachers Association
(NSTA)
Science and Children
Science for Children: Resources for Teachers
1840 Wilson Boulevard
Arlington, Virginia 22201

Phi Delta Kappa
Phi Delta Kappan
408 North Union
Bloomington, Indiana 47402

Society for Research in Music Education
Journal for Research in Music Education
c/o Music Educators National Conference
1806 Robert Fulton Drive
Reston, Virginia 22091

The Southern Poverty Law Center
Teaching Tolerance
400 Washington Avenue
Montgomery, Alabama 36104

Teachers of English to Speakers of Other
Languages (TESOL)
TESOL Newsletter
1600 Cameron Street, Suite 300
Alexandria, Virginia 22314

Drama as a Way of Knowing
Paul G. Heller
1-57110-050-4   paperback

Paul Heller is an experienced teacher, playwright, and producer who is passionate about communicating through language, drama, and music. In this engaging book he shows you how to use drama as an effective part of all classroom learning. While making it clear you don't need previous dramatic training or experience, he presents the nuts and bolts of pantomime and improvisation, of writing and acting scenes, even creating and presenting large-scale productions.

Through his Ten-Step Process in which you, the teacher, are the director, he shows what you should do to guide your students through rewarding dramatic experiences. You will see that drama is a wonderful learning tool that enables students to explore multiple dimensions of their thinking and understanding. And not only is drama academically rewarding and beneficial, it's great fun as well!

Math as a Way of Knowing
Susan Ohanian
1-57110-051-2   paperback

Award-winning author Susan Ohanian conducts a lively tour of classrooms around the country where "math time" means stimulating learning experiences. To demonstrate the point that mathematics is an active, ongoing way of perceiving and interacting with the world, she explores teaching mathematical concepts through hands-on activities; writing and talking about what numbers mean; discovering the where and why of math in everyday life; finding that there are often multiple ways to solve the same problem.

Focusing on the NCTM's *Curriculum and Evaluation Standards for School Mathematics*, Susan takes you into classrooms for a firsthand look at exciting ways the standards are implemented through innovative practices. She introduces you to new ways to organize your curriculum and classroom; suggests ways to create meaningful mathematics homework; gives you ideas to connect math across the curriculum; and links the reflective power of writing to support mathematical understanding.

For the nonspecialist in particular, Susan shows that math really is an exciting and powerful tool that students can really understand and apply in their lives.

Music as a Way of Knowing
Nick Page
1-57110-052-0   paperback

Nick Page loves to make and share music with his students, and it's likely that you will too by the time you've finished his passionate, thought-provoking book. You will also have developed a new understanding of and appreciation for the role music can play in supporting learners.

Rich with ideas on how to use music in the classroom, *Music as a Way of Knowing* will appeal especially to classroom teachers who are not musicians, but who enjoy and learn from music and want to use it with their students. Nick provides simple instructions for writing songs, using music to support learning across the curriculum, teaching singing effectively, and identifying good songs to use in the classroom.

He assures you that with time, all students can sing well. And once you've read this book, you'll have the confidence to trust yourself and your students to sing and learn well through the joy and power of music.